ISSUE 24, JUNE 2025

AUSTRALIAN FOREIGN AFFAIRS

Contributors

Zoe Jay Hawkins is a co-founder of the Tech Policy Design Institute, and a former policy adviser to cabinet ministers, government and Amazon.

Daria Impiombato is a senior analyst at the Mercator Institute for China Studies in Berlin. She was formerly with the Australian Strategic Policy Institute's cyber, technology and security section.

Robin Jeffrey is an emeritus professor of La Trobe University and the Australian National University and a non-resident senior fellow at the Institute of South Asian Studies, National University of Singapore.

Sarah Leary is an honorary First Nations foreign policy fellow at the Perth USAsia Centre and a former Australian diplomat.

Ruth McDougall is a curator and writer. Since 2003 she has worked as part of the Asia Pacific Art Department at the Queensland Art Gallery | Gallery of Modern Art.

Richard McGregor is a senior fellow at the Lowy Institute and worked in China for *The Australian* and the *Financial Times*.

Ian Verrender is the ABC's chief business correspondent.

Johanna Weaver is a co-founder of the Tech Policy Design Institute, and formerly Australia's chief cyber negotiator at the United Nations.

Australian Foreign Affairs is published three times a year by Australian Foreign Affairs Pty Ltd. Publisher: Morry Schwartz. Editor-in-chief: Erik Jensen. ISBN 978-1-76064-5854 ISSN 2208-5912 Subscriptions: 1-year print and digital subscription (3 issues): $79.00 within Australia incl. GST. 1-year digital-only auto-renew: $49.00. Payment may be made by MasterCard, Visa or Amex, or by cheque made out to Schwartz Books Pty Ltd. Payment includes postage and handling. Subscribe online at www.australianforeignaffairs.com, email subscribe@australianforeignaffairs.com or phone 1800 077 514 / 61 3 9486 0288. Correspondence should be addressed to: The Editor, Australian Foreign Affairs, 22–24 Northumberland Street, Collingwood, VIC, 3066 Australia Phone: 61 3 9486 0288 / Fax: 61 3 9486 0244 Email: enquiries@australianforeignaffairs.com. Editor: Jonathan Pearlman. Deputy Editor: Julian Welch. Associate Editor: Chris Feik. Design: Peter Long. Production Coordination: Marilyn de Castro. Typesetting: Tristan Main. Cover image: Nicolas Asfouri/AFP. Printed in Australia by McPherson's Printing Group.

Editor's Note

TECH WARS

In a speech in 2000, Bill Clinton expressed hope that his trade deal with China, which lowered tariffs and backed China's membership of the World Trade Organization, would "move China in the right direction". The aim, said the US president, was that liberalising the Chinese economy would lead to "a future of greater openness and freedom for the people of China".

It hasn't quite worked out that way. China's economy has boomed – its gross domestic product went from US$1 trillion in 2000 to US$18 trillion in 2023 – but its president, Xi Jinping, has worsened repression, restricted civil liberties and established himself as a leader for life.

In recent years, another assumption about China has been tested: that its authoritarian rule would stifle innovation and prevent it from becoming a world leader in technology. The belief was that China's state-run economy, restrictions on the internet and controls over intellectual property would constrain its creative and entrepreneurial energy. As *Time* asked in a headline in 2013, "China Makes Everything. Why Can't It Create Anything?"

In the past two decades China has invested heavily in "emerging industries" and become a world leader in various fields of technology, including renewable energy and electric vehicles. In January, the release by Chinese firm DeepSeek of a low-cost AI chatbot was described as "China's *Sputnik* moment", a breakthrough that, like the Soviet satellite launch during the Cold War, raised concerns that the United States was losing a contest with its biggest global rival.

In 1969, twelve years after the launch of *Sputnik*, America landed astronauts on the moon and won the space race. Donald Trump is hoping for a similar result in the United States' tech rivalry with China. He described the release of the DeepSeek app as "a wake-up call for our industries that we need to be laser-focused on competing to win". Along with his predecessor, Joe Biden, Trump has tried to limit Chinese technological advancement, including by imposing exports controls on semiconductors.

It is unclear whether such moves will be effective. DeepSeek, for instance, was developed using less-powerful chips than those of its US rivals and gained new efficiencies along the way. The other problem is that technology competition, unlike the space race, does not necessarily produce a clear winner. Technology evolves. DeepSeek might have marked a win for China, but, as technology experts have pointed out, the United States' AI giants will now be able to harness its breakthroughs to make new gains of their own.

For Australia, navigating this competition is about much more than the usual challenge of steering between our closest security ally and our biggest trading partner. The other challenge is that Australia is stuck in a contest whose results might be uncertain or even regressive.

At times, Australia might need to defend itself against the threat of Chinese cyber-interference and weigh the risks of permitting consumer technologies that are subject to authoritarian control. At other times, it might find itself battling US tech giants that have the White House in their corner. As always with technology, opportunities abound but they are laced with risks. Now the calculations are complicated by geopolitics.

A range of technologies – including generative AI, quantum computing, robotics and green energy – are making rapid advances and finding fresh applications. As Australia embraces the new, it must weigh its options carefully and keep checking its old assumptions.

Jonathan Pearlman

TROJAN HORSES

How to defend against Chinese technology

Richard McGregor

In early 2025, the normally staid Australian car market was upended by a surge in sales of a slick new utility vehicle. The Chinese carmaker BYD, already successfully selling its electric vehicles (EVs) locally, was overrun by demand for its "Shark 6" ute, manufactured to be sold outside of China. From a standing start, it became the sixth-biggest-selling vehicle in Australia. Buoyed by the sales, BYD predicted that within three years it could topple Toyota as the biggest-selling carmaker in the country.

In some respects, the BYD success story is just the latest variant of the Asian economic miracle washing up on Australian shores. A post-war domestic car industry once seeded by US carmakers and sheltered behind a tariff wall gradually gave way to reliable, competitive Japanese and then South Korean vehicles, with high-priced European models taking the top end of the market. The success of Chinese carmakers, according to this narrative, is nothing more than the natural outcome of the region's changing industrial and business dynamics.

In Canberra, however, where the markets are refracted through a national security lens, the rise of BYD is not just a story of a competitive car market. If you sit in our national security agencies, a car is not just a car. Nor are solar inverters, drones, wind turbines, TikTok videos and even the cranes that lift containers on our docks to be taken at face value. In the internet era, they are all, in different ways, either bundles of data or parts of industrial systems managed by software controlled by external actors.

Put another way, they are all vulnerable to unfriendly foreign intelligence agencies, which might either trawl through their data or manipulate their operations. What happens as you move closer towards some sort of regional conflict, one senior government official wondered aloud when I visited him to discuss this topic. "Could your adversary use some sort of software to shut things down or interrupt its operations? Could they render your BYD car immobile?"

The official was asking a question, to be clear, not using his query as a rhetorical device to point to a definitive conclusion. "We have to be careful about thinking, 'It's Chinese, therefore its bad,'" said another official. "You have to think about where it is in your system and what it's dependent on." But there is consensus on at least one issue in Canberra, at the bureaucratic and political level: China has the capability and intent of pulling in huge data sets and unpacking them for intelligence purposes.

It doesn't matter whether the Chinese company is part of the state or privately owned. According to Chinese law, companies of any colour in China must comply with intelligence directives from state security. There is no system of warrants or judicial review in China's joined-up party-state. "Assume the worst," said Mike Pezzullo, the former head of the Department of Home Affairs. "They can operate at scale. Their capabilities are not primitive. You would be a mug to think they are not applying their skills at scale in espionage."

Xi Jinping has made it crystal clear in recent years that private tech companies must be aligned with his political objectives. Jack Ma, the billionaire founder of Alibaba, was forced out of his company after he repeatedly challenged regulators. Other senior executives resigned after Xi launched a campaign to discipline local tech giants in 2019. Even foreign companies such as Apple are facing measures to force them to keep their knowhow on the ground in China. The Chinese government has impeded efforts by Foxconn, the Taiwanese company that makes iPhones for Apple, to export machinery to India to diversify its supply chain.

The problems with industrial systems go deeper than just the ability to manipulate their operations through ostensibly commercial software updates. Since 2023, the United States has tracked a group of Chinese state-sponsored hackers, known as Volt Typhoon, which has used malicious software to penetrate communications, energy, transport and water systems in the US and its territories, some of which, such as Guam, are bases for its military.

Australia is vulnerable to the same threat. "It is worth us thinking about a near-conflict scenario: what would the adversary actually do?" said one government official. "If we think they have penetrated our critical infrastructure, would they bother meddling with consumer vehicles? If you can take out the electricity grid and stuff up the water systems, do you have to piss around with all the rest of it? To stop force projection, you might just turn the water off."

Australian officials have watched as hackers from countries such as China and Russia have probed and mapped our networks. The hackers then hoard that knowhow, ready to get back into the networks when they want to disable them. The officials are acutely aware that Australia has never been hit by a high-impact cyber attack from a nation-state. "Imagine if the entire payments system went out – if all phone providers went out," said one official. "It would be government-ending."

Computers on wheels

To understand the sorts of difficulties that lie ahead for smaller countries, it is worth revisiting the two headline-grabbing decisions Australia has taken on Chinese tech. China was furious about the Julia Gillard government's 2012 decision to keep Chinese companies, including Huawei, out of the building of the National Broadband Network (NBN), but the decision hardly upended bilateral relations. Two years later, President Xi Jinping visited Australia, his first and only trip here as head of the Communist Party (and thus leader of the country), and addressed a joint sitting of parliament. In the same year, Australia and China signed a trade agreement. As Tony Abbott, who hosted Xi, remarked sardonically in private at the time, Australia's relations with China were a mix of "fear and greed".

By 2018, when Malcolm Turnbull banned Huawei from building Australia's 5G network, fear was coming to the fore. The 5G decision was very different from the NBN one. With the NBN, Chinese companies were up against several other competitive bidders. With 5G, not only were the Chinese offering a cheaper price, Huawei had the best technology as well. The 5G ban, a global first for Canberra, was a tipping point for China's negative view of Australia, and a major cause of the punitive trade measures that Beijing imposed in 2020.

Difficult and controversial at the time, it is remarkable now to see the almost universal support and indeed enthusiasm for the ban across the political spectrum. Scott Morrison and Peter Dutton, ministers in the Turnbull cabinet, have jostled in recent years to claim credit for forcing what was then a tough decision. Morrison announced the decision as acting minister for Home Affairs, but only because Dutton had resigned to challenge for the leadership a few days earlier. Most insiders credit Turnbull and the head of the Australian Signals Directive (and now ASIO chief), Mike Burgess, and his staff as the prime drivers in the Huawei ban.

Hindsight is easy, and all politicians try to rewrite history in their favour. But in retrospect the Huawei ban was not the end point it seemed at the time. Rather, it was the start of a long march through an increasingly treacherous global tech battlefield. The reality is sinking in for Canberra that the decisions only get harder from now on. To illustrate why, let's go back to BYD.

The United States, Europe and Canada have put high tariffs on Chinese EVs to protect their car industries. Australia, however, has had nothing left to protect since the Abbott government cut subsidies to multinational car companies in 2013 and they shut the last of their local factories. Australia tilts the car market's playing field slightly on climate change grounds, by offering incentives to buy EVs. Otherwise, the government's approach has been to ignore complaints that Chinese manufacturers benefit from unfair subsidies at home. Australia has been happy to leave consumers to chase the best cars at the cheapest prices. Increasingly, that means they are buying Chinese. About 80 per cent of the EVs sold in Australia are made in China, including Teslas, which come from a factory in Shanghai. Volvo, which makes the Polestar EV, is probably still associated with Sweden, where it was founded, in the minds of most Australians, but it has been owned by a private Chinese company, Geely, since 2010.

In security-speak, however, Australians aren't buying cars, they are buying "connected vehicles". The modern car is a computer on wheels, with sophisticated sensor systems that detect not just traffic but also, potentially, the faces of people it passes and the driving habits and locations of its owner. All of this can be passed back to a central network, which, if not actually in China, can at least be accessed from China. "You could have mobile surveillance vans at scale. What would happen if one was able to drive through a sensitive government car park in Canberra and harvest all the number plates?" asked a government adviser. The Chinese authorities have the ability to go straight to the manufacturer. In other words, there is no barrier to accessing the data. "That's the real concern."

In the case of 5G, there was little to no Huawei equipment in the network in Australia. That wasn't the case for the United Kingdom, for example, which only agreed to remove Huawei from their networks under immense pressure from the United States. Germany faced the same issue. In both cases, the rip-and-replace policy was an expensive, politically contested, diplomatically draining and time-consuming undertaking. Imagine applying the same policy to cars, solar inverters and the many other software-driven devices that originate in China and are embedded in the Australian consumer and industrial economies.

In 2018, Telstra, Vodaphone and Optus hadn't rolled out 5G infrastructure of any substance. Thus, making a binary policy intervention wasn't that difficult. Fast-forward only a few years and even the most cursory examination of the markets for cars, solar inverters, commercial drones and other technologies underline the challenges thrown up by Chinese dominance.

To make a black-and-white decision on the market now would have a massive impact on millions of consumers and businesses, which would have to pay to retrofit industrial systems or modify the types of cars allowed on our roads. "Looking back, 5G was quite an easy decision, although it didn't feel like that at the time," said one government official. "Now, there would be a bigger impact from intervention, but the case for intervention is less clear."

Several politicians and senior public servants raised the case of solar panels. What if the Americans choose to put enormous tariffs on solar panels to protect their own industry? We don't have an industry of our own. So why shouldn't we take advantage of cheap prices from China, which dominates the sector? That seems largely uncontroversial. But solar inverters, along with multiple other products that capture huge amounts of data, are different. In May 2025, for instance, Reuters reported that US officials had discovered undocumented communications devices in Chinese-made solar inverters.

At the other end of the spectrum are wind turbines. Would Australia, one former politician asks, have the same attitude towards Goldwind, the wind turbine manufacturer headquartered in Beijing, whose software is written and upgraded in China, as we would to the Danish firm Vestas? "Do we lie awake at night worrying about the malign influence of the Kingdom of Denmark? No," said the politician.

Until 2018, Australia seemed to have a comforting template to handle the tech security threat from what Canberra euphemistically calls "untrusted vendors" – largely code for China. After both the 2012 and 2018 decisions, Australia survived China's immense diplomatic wrath. Throughout these controversies, the Americans either stood to the side and applauded the decisions or backed Australia in with offers to maintain privileged access to their own tech universe.

Such a framework is unlikely to hold in the future. The consumer goods and industrial systems that sit at the heart of the economy in Australia are just about all made in China. That means multiple products and industrial systems could be subject to national security reviews and assessed for vulnerabilities, a massive and fraught regulatory task. "If China dominates the market for technology, it becomes a scale problem," said Simeon Gilding, one of the architects of the 5G ban, and formerly at the Australian Signals Directorate.

Diplomatically difficult at the time, the 5G decision looks easy in retrospect, as the Turnbull government didn't have to dismantle existing networks to enforce the policy. They simply set conditions for a new system that was yet to be built. Now, entire consumer and industrial systems would be up for review.

The superpower squeeze

China is not the only reason Canberra is getting anxious about the global tech wars. Donald Trump's whirlwind opening to his second term, in which he attacked friends and embraced enemies, sent shudders through the political and bureaucratic establishment in the Australian capital. Beijing has form in coercing Australia, and we have already started to develop the muscle memory to fend it off. But as Trump makes clear, naked American coercion could be coming as well. As a technology price taker, Australia might find itself having to manage both sides of the argument. In the words of a senior government official, "Australia is stuck in the middle between two superpowers who are using tech as a vehicle for competition."

The parameters and depth of US–China tech competition have become increasingly well defined in recent years. President Joe Biden's national security advisor, Jake Sullivan, described the administration's policy as erecting "a small yard and a high fence". In other words, the United States would put a protective barrier around a core of heavily restricted products, technologies and business activities, many with potential military applications. As well as cutting off Chinese access to its own high-tech armoury, Washington has pressured partners such as Japan, South Korea, Taiwan and the Netherlands, whose companies controlled key technologies in the semiconductor supply chain, not to sell to its adversaries. Washington also curbed investment in sensitive sectors, both by US companies in China and by Chinese companies in the United States. In late March 2025 Trump toughened restrictions on Chinese access to US technology, adding scores of companies to a blacklist on national security grounds.

As Trump makes clear, naked American coercion could be coming

For its part, China has always seen tech as a key battleground with the United States. From the early days of market-driven economic development in the 1980s, Chinese leaders worried about being too reliant on Western technologies. Gradually, through a combination of protectionism, investment and industrial-scale theft of intellectual property, Beijing chipped away at foreign technology dominance. Xi Jinping has turbocharged that trend, putting what he calls "high-quality growth" at the heart of his economic strategy. Xi has spent, and continues to spend, tens of billions of dollars in an effort to shift businesses out of traditional growth drivers such as building infrastructure and low-margin, low-cost manufacturing and into new frontier industries.

At forums like Davos, Xi preaches to the choir, talking up free trade and "win-win cooperation". At home, he strikes a different tone, emphasising the need for China to dominate key technologies, materials and industries. He has told his officials that he wants "an assassin's mace" to give Beijing "deterrent capabilities" against foreigners, should they impose sanctions on China. In short, he wants China to have the ability to do to America what he thinks America is trying to do China.

China is also clear about its aim to be the biggest provider of technology and industrial systems to foreign markets, especially South-East Asia. In part, this is the kind of normal competition that nations and companies have always engaged in. In China's case, it is also about regional diplomatic ascendency. In the words of local scholars, China wants its companies to control the "hard connectivity of infrastructure", the "soft interoperability of rules and standards" and the "chain connectivity of industrial structure" in the region. In other words, Beijing wants to ensure its companies have access to, and the ability to manage, the entire tech system in our near abroad.

In some quarters in Australia, to even talk about hedging between rival superpowers in a global tech war is heresy. The preponderant view in the national security establishment is that Australia should and will support the United States in any contest with China, both for practical and ideological reasons. Not only do we have a longstanding alliance, which is the foundation of our foreign policy. We are also military and intelligence partners, deeply connected through years of technology, information and personnel exchanges. Those relationships have built a level of intimacy and trust that the Chinese are incapable of replicating – and they probably have no desire to replicate it anyway. The American military and intelligence establishments continue to value such ties with Australia and like-minded partners. Trump 2.0, however, not so much.

American peril

The Trump White House exhibited scant regard for the interests of longstanding partners in its early months in office. Europe, Canada, Mexico, Denmark and Japan have all faced demands from the president, some of which impinge on their sovereignty, with no sense that the deep ties they have nurtured with the United States over years will act as a restraint. The naked intimidation that is already becoming the hallmark of Trump's second term was on display in February 2025 when Secretary of Commerce Howard Lutnick addressed Treasurer Jim Chalmers and Australian superannuation fund chiefs at a gathering in Washington DC to burnish the nation's credentials.

The former Wall Street trader made clear that Washington expected Canberra's unqualified support if the United States and China locked horns in an economic war or worse. Everyone in the room left with the understanding that the Americans might one day demand that Australia cut its trade ties with China, a country that takes more than a third of our exports. Cast aside was the fact that the United States had just imposed tariffs on Australian steel and aluminium, in contravention of the two countries' free trade pact. Also cast aside was the fact that Australia excels on Trump's personal metric for judging foreign countries' worth to the United States, with a bilateral trade balance heavily in America's favour. In other words, when Trump says jump, Australia should jump.

In April, Trump added further tariffs on Australian imports, albeit at the low end of global imposts. Later, administration officials floated a proposal to lift tariffs on selected countries, on the condition that they join the United States in imposing trade restrictions on Chinese goods. Beijing, in turn, threatened to retaliate against both the United States and its partners if this happened.

Lutnick's in-your-face swagger reinforced a second instinct in Canberra: to try to distinguish between American demands that encapsulate genuine security concerns and those that are just protectionism in disguise, with security concerns deployed as a catch-all excuse. Much of Trump's early trade policy fits into a related third category. Trump 2.0 has a broader definition of security, measuring the import of any economic decision by whether it helps or hinders the president's plans to revive manufacturing in the United States.

Malcolm Turnbull is one of many prominent Australians wondering about the wisdom of Australia being so closely aligned with the United States. "The United States under President Trump does not share the values we have shared with every single one of his predecessors, Republican and Democrat, for over eighty years. And he does not pretend to share them. This is a feature, not a bug of the Trump administration," Turnbull said at summit of foreign policy experts he convened in Canberra in April. "Australian sovereignty, sovereign autonomy, has never been so important. And yet in recent years it has never been so diminished."

Over time, the shared interests that bind us together could start to crack as well. In the words of Gilding, the former signals intelligence official, "If we don't have some kind of shared interests with the US, then getting our tech nobbled is the least of our problems."

Much of the debate in Australia focuses on Chinese law and its licence to force its companies to hand over data. But Australian government agencies are often also concerned about the data that US tech giants, such as Meta and Google, aggregate. A foreign intelligence service, for example, could go to a third-party broker and buy legally as much data as they want from Meta. "There's often a dichotomy presented of Western tech good, Chinese tech bad. I think it is much more complicated than that."

The collection of data is ubiquitous in today's world, going far beyond what most consumers probably realise. The Australian consumer magazine *Choice* recently surveyed the multitude of ways companies hoover up customers' data with a view to selling it back into the commercial marketplace, including to foreign buyers. One section was headlined "What your robot vacuum cleaner knows about you".

Reducing the risk

Each Chinese tech and social media advance comes with a new challenge. For a while, some Australian politicians advocated banning TikTok, as the US Congress has tried to do, because of the dangers arising from data harvesting and the manipulation of its algorithm. But the absence of a smoking gun tying Beijing to the management of the app, as well as TikTok's popularity, soon made most politicians drop that idea. The same goes in different ways for WeChat, China's ubiquitous all-in-one messaging app, and Red Note, a newer social media connector. Like TikTok, both have become unbannable, in no small part because Australian politicians use them to communicate with their Chinese Australian constituents, who in turn have told them they are indispensable for doing business with China.

In late 2024 Chinese researchers announced a major AI breakthrough, DeepSeek, which was able to closely replicate the most advanced Western platforms at much less cost. Once again, calls came in Australia for it to be banned, but these were soon scaled back to a directive that it not be used on government devices. Within weeks, DeepSeek was being incorporated into BYD's driver-assistance technology for its vehicles in China. The so-called "God's Eye" system isn't yet on the Shark 6 but it can't be far off. In other words, DeepSeek could be soon sharpening its instincts by training on data gathered in Australia.

The United States has already laid down a mark on so-called connected vehicles. In Washington, the benefits of connecting vehicles to the internet – it helps train the cars to make them smarter and safer – are now weighed against the downsides: that foreign countries can harvest data and potentially take over remote-control systems. After an extensive review process, the Biden administration, in its final week in office, issued a rule banning the sale and import of cars that use hardware or software and autonomous driving systems produced by "entities subject to the jurisdiction" of China and Russia. The ban will start in 2027. Put another way, the BYD Shark 6 ute will not get a look in the US small trucks market, no matter how good it is.

The United States has been very aggressive, in the words of one Australian official, "in looking at anything with a wire that ends up in China". Anthony Albanese's government has been much quieter about how it is approaching these issues, just as it has been quieter about our differences with China more generally. On 20 December 2024, the Home Affairs department released a document titled "Technology Vendor Review Framework" to guide policy on the adoption of foreign technologies. Released days before Christmas, the document was designed to be buried amid the summer holiday torpor, and that was how it panned out. The announcement got little coverage. "The document was meant to be about signalling," said one government adviser. "But if you don't talk about the issue, there is no signalling."

National security officials warn that storing data onshore is not a failsafe panacea

The strategy for managing technology on national security grounds can be divided into three headings: triage, mitigate, ban. All three could be applied to connected cars. You can restrict government from owning the cars. You can stop them from being used in critical infrastructure. You can attempt to have the data stored onshore, which seems to be the all-purpose, off-the-shelf solution to the problem of China gathering and using data.

The United States has its own version of a domestic storage policy, "Project Texas", so called because the data centres are in Texas. The policy was initially designed to allow TikTok to continue operating in the United States, by having the US software company Oracle manage and oversee its US-generated data. Canberra has studied piggybacking on the US initiative, while also looking at whether it is possible to do something similar in Australia. But national security officials warn that storing data onshore is not a failsafe panacea. Formally, data could be quarantined within national boundaries, but shadow copies could be made and sent offshore. The data could be hacked. Circuit boards at the data centre could be programmed to store it or send it on to third parties.

Some Canberra mandarins support replicating the policy used to screen investment in critical infrastructure to handle the kinds of choices Australia faces in discriminating between technologies. Pezzullo, the former Home Affairs chief, advocates drawing up a list of technologies, or sectors, of cascading importance. You have a "decoupling" checklist, in other words, a ban and a "derisking" checklist, which imposes limits and conditions. The aim would be to have, in effect, two technical systems. "Short of a change in governance in China, we cannot have any deep technological relationship with them," he says. Pezzullo admits, however, that technology is not like critical infrastructure. "It does not lend itself to a clean separation of technologies."

Most of the officials interviewed for this article said that the idea that Australia could protect itself by building a clean internet is a fantasy. Even European and US companies such as Nokia, Ericsson and Cisco have Chinese parts or technology in them. And all systems can be hacked, even if that doesn't necessarily deliver the intruder enduring access. "Anyone who thinks you can divide technologies and have a Western internet and an authoritarian internet is having themselves on," said one official. "You can't mitigate this to zero. The key is reducing the time to detect and the time to respond. Find it quickly and resolve it quickly."

Canberra divides the world into layers of sensitivity. The government has to give top priority to protecting the most sensitive functions of the system: ministerial decision-making, intelligence and defence. Government services are important, with one-third of the economy being social security. "We will intervene at a high level; not just the economic level," said one official.

But the big policy conundrum – how to create trust with untrusted partners and/or their products – is far off. There is no roadmap for what lies ahead, not even one mapped by BYD's Shark 6, now being described as "Australia's favourite ute". ■

SYSTEM UPDATE

An Australian-led new deal for tech

Johanna Weaver & Zoe Jay Hawkins

Many expected Beijing to redraw the international rules-based order. Few anticipated that Washington, led by a US president enabled by a small group of tech billionaires, would seize the pen.

US global leadership is disintegrating, loudly and in plain sight. This has serious ramifications for how democracies such as Australia should conceive of their role on the world stage. And, whether visible or not, technology is at the epicentre of the contest for the new world order.

The last time the world order was remade, Australia helped write the rules. At the 1945 San Francisco Conference, at which the United Nations Charter was forged, Australia's H.V. Evatt was hailed as "a leading statesman for the world's conscience". It marked the birth of Australian middle-power diplomacy.

While the geopolitical and technical transformations we are living through are seismic, it is not inevitable that the world will be remade in

Washington or Beijing's image. Australia has agency in how this story unfolds. And Australia is better placed than most countries to help shape both the global rules and the technologies that will define the decades ahead. But first we must accept that the world has changed.

Regime change in the United States

Anne Applebaum at *The Atlantic* put it bluntly: what's happening in the United States isn't a shift in policy, it's "regime change". *Wired* has described it as a "digital coup". Donald Trump, backed by Elon Musk and the so-called Department of Government Efficiency (DOGE), is working to dismantle the very machinery of the United States federal government.

USAID, the State Department, the Department of Education, the Environmental Protection Agency and the Office of Personnel Management are just a few of the agencies and departments being gutted. The implications of what is happening at each agency are profound, but let's focus on one. Shuttering USAID is a hammer blow to US global soft power. Even if funding freezes are reversed, the United States has placed itself in the "unreliable partner" column. In the meantime, who steps in to feed starving populations or deliver maternal and child healthcare? Some countries in the Indo-Pacific may turn to Australia as their "partner of choice". But many more will turn to Beijing, especially without a significant increase in Australia's aid budget.

While China's Xi Jinping may be rubbing his hands with glee at this US own goal, back in Washington the Trump administration has granted DOGE access to an expanding list of US government IT systems, including the Department of the Treasury, the Internal Revenue Service, the Social Security Administration and the Department of Labor.

DOGE was formally established by executive order by Trump on his first day but, despite its name, does not have the status of a cabinet-level government department. The name is an inside joke drawn from an internet meme and cryptocurrency that began as a misspelling of "dog" in a cartoon. (Yes, really.) According to President Trump, Musk is in charge of DOGE but, according to the White House, Musk isn't employed by DOGE. Contrary to standard practice for senior political appointments, Musk has not been confirmed by the Senate. There is no indication that he or any of his DOGE team – mostly young men, all devotees of Musk – have been security-cleared. Meanwhile, Musk and his companies have glaring conflicts of interest, from competing for lucrative government contracts to being subject to the very regulations they may now influence from the inside.

Personality differences aside, Trump's installation of Musk in such a role is the equivalent of Prime Minister Anthony Albanese handing Mike Cannon-Brookes unfettered access to the Australian Taxation Office, Services Australia (including the Centrelink and Medicare payment systems), the Australian Government Security Vetting Agency, the Department of Home Affairs, Border Force and the Treasury – and with no oversight or accountability.

Maybe Musk moves on. Maybe he and Trump have a bust-up. Maybe the courts step in, and maybe Trump respects court orders. But even if reason prevails, the damage to the US government's IT systems has been done, and it's irreversible. There is credible speculation that Musk has exfiltrated large amount of data. It is hard to believe Musk and his team have not installed "back doors" to maintain access long after his formal work is done. Deletion or alteration of government records can also not be discounted. It could take years to understand what Musk and his DOGE team have accessed, modified or exfiltrated – if we ever do (whistleblowers claim the audit trails are being deleted in parallel). But what is clear is this: any system Musk and DOGE have touched can no longer be considered secure. And the data on these systems can no longer be considered private. In a digital-first world, this amounts to the subversion of the machinery of an independent public service, a cornerstone of modern democratic governance.

The Trump administration is blurring the lines between the public service and private empire

But it doesn't stop there. Having been given access to government systems, Musk and DOGE, backed by yet another executive order, are pushing to merge citizen data held across agencies into a single, centralised mega-database. Undoubtably there are efficiencies to be gained from bringing different government data sets together, and many democracies, including Australia, are pursuing data sharing across agencies for improved services. However, under this administration, such a mega-database could be misused at scale and in Orwellian ways, leading to unprecedented domestic surveillance. Unless strong protections are built into the system, the efficiencies of this centralisation will come at the cost of fundamental rights. It is the value placed on the second over the first that separates a liberal democracy from a startup, or an authoritarian regime.

Combine DOGE's activities with the Trump administration's disregard for the Supreme Court, its campaign to roll back civil rights, its attacks on universities and its retrenching of large numbers of federal civil servants, and an alarming picture of democratic decline emerges.

A professional, independent public service that is empowered to act in the service of the public – as distinct from simply pursuing the interests of the party in power – is one of Australia's greatest assets. So too are our often clunky but functional digital systems, which deliver some of the best government services in the world. Australia has a non-politicised judiciary and an executive and legislature that respect the doctrine of separation of powers. These are not small things. We should value them more than we do, and defend them fiercely.

By contrast, in the United States, the Trump administration, enabled by Musk and DOGE, is blurring the lines between the public service and private empire. This is at odds with the free world's belief in democratic restraint: the notion that even the most powerful must remain accountable to the people, and that power should be constrained by law, not wielded at whim. The United States remains a global power but is no longer the leader of the free world. That position is now vacant. This raises urgent questions about how Australia defines our role in global affairs.

Tech firms trump state power

For centuries, the international order has rested – at least nominally – on the Westphalian principle that states have the exclusive right to govern within their borders, free from outside interference. It's a principle so foundational to modern statehood that we often forget it exists. But from the early 1990s, with the export of the internet (and, with it, US values), the idea that states had the exclusive right to govern global technology within their borders became a point of contention.

Until recently, the popular wisdom was that if every country imposed discrete domestic rules, it would "break the internet", undermining its globally interoperable nature. The concept of "digital sovereignty" was – and, for many, remains – the calling card of authoritarian governments defending their use of technology to repress and control their populations.

As Vili Lehdonvirta documents in *Cloud Empires: How Digital Platforms Are Overtaking the State and How We Can Regain Control,* powers typically reserved by governments (such as operating public infrastructure, overseeing markets, creating and enforcing social rules – community guidelines, content moderation, codes of conduct) have in many cases been outsourced to private tech companies. Comfortable that US values aligned with their own, and wary of inhibiting the economic promise of the technologies, Western governments ceded this sovereign power with little protest and often with little regulatory constraint, if any. Tech companies accepted this gift with relish, doing right by their shareholders, while often – but not always – delivering positive impacts for their customers.

The result has transformed modern life. From social platforms evolving into the modern public square (Facebook, X, TikTok) to services powering consumer revolutions in AI efficiencies (ChatGPT, DeepSeek), enabling trade and export (Amazon, Alibaba), helping us find our way around (Google Maps) and make payments (WeChat), tech companies are behind services that we engage with every day. Some of these companies even operate the cloud – large servers that facilitate remote and elastic access to data and software, and that compute at scale – that underpins governments, services and enterprises around the world.

This transfer of power has also introduced harms that governments have been ill-equipped to manage, especially as their and their citizens' dependence on these technologies increased. This means that, today, the Westphalian compact is being undermined not just by rival states – as we see with Russia's invasion of Ukraine – but by certain companies that have more users than most countries have citizens. These companies also have bigger annual turnover than many nations' GDP, and as a result more influence on world affairs than many governments.

In recognition of this, some governments have asserted their right to regulate technology within their borders. Countries have passed legislation requiring tech companies to comply with rules across a range of topics: from online safety (Australia, the United Kingdom, the European Union, South Korea) and local content requirements for streaming services (Canada, France) to privacy and data protection (India, Indonesia) and algorithmic transparency (the European Union, Canada).

This trend proves that the tech sector can – and should – be regulated like any other.

In some instances, this pushback has met a formidable obstacle: platform non-compliance. In April 2025, in its first use of new regulatory powers, the European Union slapped Apple and Meta with fines of €500 million and €200 million, respectively, for failing to comply with competition and user choice provisions under the region's *Digital Markets Act*. The White House labelled the fines "economic extortion" that the United States "will not tolerate", further complicating an already complex enforcement challenge.

Some companies push back with more attitude than others. Elon Musk's opposition to the Australian eSafety Commissioner's direction to social media platform X to take down videos of the 2024 Wakeley church stabbing attack prompted Prime Minister Albanese to say, "We'll do what's necessary to take on this arrogant billionaire who thinks he's above the law, but also above common decency."

This face-off between government and big tech has been brewing for many years but, under Trump 2.0 some US tech firms are now being supported by state-backed coercion. The Trump administration has threatened tariff retaliation or even US withdrawal from NATO if countries impose regulations that "could inhibit the growth or intended operation of United States companies". For governments, navigating how to hold foreign tech giants accountable without being cut off from the internet's essential arteries – already a difficult task – is now also dangerous. The United States has always held significant leverage over other countries in light of its financial, security and technological clout. US investments, like those from China, have always had strings attached, but Trump's administration is demonstrating an unprecedented appetite to openly exploit this leverage.

The European Union has the market power to stand up to Trump's threats. In April 2025, European Commission president Ursula von der Leyen asserted that the EU's digital rules "must be enforced ... We don't care where a company's from and who's running it." The Commission is competing fiercely for global science talent, with Von der Leyen announcing the new "Choose Europe" initiative, paired with €500 million for 2025–27, to "make Europe the home of innovation again". The EU market has also started conversations about de-risking digital infrastructure. *The Register* reports "Europe's cloud customers eyeing exit from US hyperscalers", with CEO of UK cloud provider CIVO Mark Boost reflecting: "There are three factors. The first is really the unreliability, because we see what Trump is doing and the danger that things will be just switched off from one day to another for negotiation purposes. Then we see the whole question around pricing with the tariffs. And then the other thing is really the espionage factor. This is relatively new and surprising to me ... but now you see what Musk is doing, that you can access really confidential databases ... I think this is a realistic fear nowadays."

Analogous surveillance and security concerns were the driving force behind Australia and other countries' decision to ban Huawei from their 5G mobile networks. While such accounts from US competitors are undoubtedly inflated by vested interests, if companies in Europe are exploring options to diversify, imagine the debates in Jakarta, Nairobi or Brasilia – places even warier of being caught in the digital crossfire between Washington and Beijing.

Geoeconomic bullying risks nudging allies and fence-sitters alike into the arms of alternative providers. For some, like Europe, that may mean another desperate attempt at raising domestic champions. For others it will mean China. This matters not just because authoritarian tech encodes authoritarian values, but because the shape of global infrastructure determines the shape of global power. The more countries rely on Chinese cloud, cables, satellites, chips, AI models, platforms and services, the more leverage Beijing will accrue over everything from surveillance to trade.

This sovereignty struggle creates challenges for Australia. Domestically, we must determine how to regulate global platforms without incurring punitive backlash. Internationally, we need to adjust to the new operating environment in which our foreign policy takes shape. The soft-power halo around American tech (to the extent it survived the Snowden revelations) has served as a modest asset in liberal diplomacy. But the United States' halo has slipped, and as a result some countries will be reassessing their foreign technology dependencies.

Navigating the US–China AI battle

For those "inside the beltway", in Washington DC or Beijing, or huddled in Five Eyes security briefings (or perhaps reading this journal with a glass of shiraz in hand), AI has become synonymous with geopolitical competition. But for most countries AI is interesting because of the innovative possibilities it unlocks: better healthcare, more resilient infrastructure, natural disaster mitigations, language translation.

It is notable, for example, that optimism regarding the potential use of AI is much higher in countries across the region than in Australia: 69 per cent and 55 per cent of people in China and India, respectively, see AI products and services as offering more benefits than risks, according to research by the University of Melbourne. In Australia, only 30 per cent say the same (the lowest of forty-seven countries surveyed).

The value of AI lies in its promise to solve the greatest challenges of our time. In US foreign policy, however, that promise has increasingly been obscured by the race for strategic advantage. The competition for resources – accelerators, data, data centres, models and scalable businesses – is undeniably fierce. On his second day in office, Trump issued an executive order with the stated aim of "enhancing America's global AI dominance".

The AI race is multi-level. First, it is a fight to create and control the world's most powerful semiconductor chips, referred to as "accelerators". Second, there is the race to use these accelerators to develop the most powerful frontier AI models. Third, the challenge is to deploy these models via the global network of "hyperscaler" digital infrastructure that underpins economic and political systems around the world. Fourth – though now seemingly out of fashion – there is the race to "hold the pen" on global governance for AI's safe and responsible use.

While the US government has largely checked out of the governance debate, it's doubling down on export controls. The accelerator market is dominated by US-owned Nvidia, which holds a staggering 80 per cent or so of the global market. To maintain this edge, the US government has implemented strict export controls on the most advanced accelerators – such as Nvidia's H100 chips – from reaching China. While they have undoubtedly slowed China's progress, these restrictions have failed to prevent – and may in fact have encouraged – a different kind of domestic innovation. In early 2025, the Chinese firm DeepSeek released a reasoning language model – DeepSeek-R1 – that reportedly rivals US frontier models on some benchmarks but was trained on a fraction of the compute power. These claims are contested but the signal is clear: you can't prevent all innovation through restrictions. According to Stanford University, while the United States still leads in the *quantity* of top-tier AI models (with forty), the *performance* gap is narrowing – and China is innovating under constraints.

America's attempt to ring-fence its AI innovation appears to be having unintended consequences

America's changing AI export controls have global reach and lasting reverberations. In May 2025 the US Department of Commerce rescinded Biden's controversial AI Diffusion Framework – which proposed to categorise countries into three "tiers" of access to US AI technologies – just days before it was due to come into force. The

Trump administration has indicated plans to replace it with a "simpler rule" aimed at promoting US AI dominance, but no specific alternative has yet been put forward. *Bloomberg* reporting suggests that the new US approach may involve direct negotiations with individual countries. In the same announcement, the US government also warned that Chinese Huawei Ascend chips were likely produced in violation of US export controls, and therefore their use "anywhere in the world" may enliven US enforcement action – increasing pressure on countries to choose between the United States and China.

In parallel, Trump and Musk embarked on a co-presidential tour of the Middle East, accompanied by several US tech company CEOs. Trump announced plans to allow the United Arab Emirates to import 500,000 of Nvidia's most advanced AI chips annually, with 100,000 chips slated to go to Emirati tech firm G42 each year – notwithstanding concerns reported during the Biden administration that G42 might have been siphoning advanced American technology to Chinese companies. On the same trip, at the Saudi–US Investment Forum, over US$600 billion in US–Saudi investment deals were announced, including a collaboration between Nvidia and Saudi-backed AI firm Humain to establish AI facilities powered by US chips.

But, in a domain where infrastructure build times span years and AI investments create long-term dependencies, countries need more than just access to cutting-edge technology today – they need confidence that their access will remain stable and not change without warning. Beijing has leaned into a more permissive, and at times strategically open-source, posture. Since mid-2023, Chinese firms have been contributing prolifically to Hugging Face and GitHub, the world's most prominent platforms for sharing and collaborating on code and machine-learning models. Notably, Chinese developers have released open-source variants of large language models such as Yi and DeepSeek, and modified versions of Meta's Llama, providing enough information about the model and how it was created for Chinese innovation to be replicated by others. Deviating from US firms' proprietary approach is a calculated bid to shape the AI ecosystem in the Global South. By lowering the barrier to entry, in terms of licensing costs, compute and export restrictions, China is offering a pathway for countries to gain access to powerful AI models.

But China's diffusion strategy extends well beyond AI models. Under the banner of its Digital Silk Road, Beijing is funding and building AI-relevant infrastructure – from data centres and cloud computing hubs to smart city systems and satellite networks – across Asia, Africa, the Middle East and Latin America. Partnerships in Kenya, Brazil and the UAE have included joint AI research labs, hardware deployment and talent training programs. For many governments, this non-discriminatory approach and holistic combination of technical support and financing makes China a more predictable and accessible technology partner.

America's recent attempt to control AI appears to be having unintended consequences. First, it has not prevented Chinese innovation in AI – and, arguably, these new Middle East deals could provide a conduit for China to access advanced US chips. Second, Washington's transactional approach of diffusion by deal-making, and its policy of penalising those that use Chinese tech, may further alienate countries lacking deep pockets to "do a deal" with Trump – pushing them towards China's more accessible and affordable technology. Third, it misses an opportunity to meet the more practical needs of countries looking to leverage AI innovation for public benefit. In regions where building sovereign AI from scratch is out of reach, the availability, affordability and accessibility of Chinese-origin models can make them an attractive alternative. Many countries are asking a practical question: where can we get AI models that work for us? Pacific island nations, for example, where climate change is the greatest national security threat, want access to tools that don't require data centres the size of small towns. By innovating under constraints, lowering barriers through open source and offering comparative consistency, China is not only accelerating its AI diffusion, it's exporting influence.

Against that backdrop, it makes strategic and economic sense for Australia to position itself as a trusted, reliable provider of responsible AI for the public good. Countries in our region want access to AI to solve real-world problems. This will rarely require access to the most cutting-edge AI frontier models, but it does require better tech than many have access to today. Australia should foster a domestic AI industry that specialises in consistently deploying cost-effective, energy-efficient and regionally accessible AI. In doing this, we will meet a real need in the region while not ceding the space to China.

Paying without the greenback

Aside from imposing controls over semiconductors or AI accelerators, Trump has also focused attention on one other major chokepoint: the global financial system.

The United States wields significant power (including the ability to enforce sanctions) because the US dollar (USD) is the preferred currency for global transactions, and the United States has de facto control of technical systems that facilitate global flows of USD. Rather than constantly change large volumes of currencies (which takes time and costs money), countries hold foreign currency reserves, which they use to facilitate international payments. According to IMF data from April 2025, around 60 per cent of global foreign exchange reserves are held in USD, compared to 20 per cent in euros and just 2 per cent in Chinese yuan (and 2 per cent in Australian dollars).

Almost all large-scale USD transactions are facilitated by the Society for Worldwide Interbank Financial Telecommunication (SWIFT) and cleared though the Clearing House Interbank Payments System (CHIPS) or Fedwire. Without access to USD, SWIFT and CHIPS or Fedwire, it is extremely challenging to do business across borders.

The power this gives the United States has long made countries like China, Russia and Iran uneasy. This escalated to alarm in 2022 when the United States and the European Union blocked Russian banks from SWIFT and froze large amount of Russia's USD currency reserves in response to Russia's invasion of Ukraine. Of course, countries – including Russia – had been sanctioned before. However, until 2022, blocking

SWIFT and freezing the USD reserves of a G8 economy had been considered by many – including, reportedly, China – as unthinkable: taking so much currency out of circulation risked breaking the interconnected global economy. The economy didn't break, but confidence in the "global" financial plumbing was irreparably shaken. Since then, Trump's "nothing is off the table" approach to advancing US interests has only deepened concern and sent countries scrambling to find alternative means to facilitate cross-border payments and to diversify their foreign currency reserves.

What is extraordinary is that there are currently no viable global alternatives. China has developed an alternative to SWIFT, the Cross-Border Interbank Payment System (CIPS). However, CIPS transactions are settled in yuan, and China's strict capital controls, combined with concerns about the Chinese Communist Party's extrajudicial influence over assets in its jurisdiction, make it unlikely that CIPS and the yuan will displace SWIFT and USD primacy – at least in the near term.

Outside the United States, there is growing interest in cross-border payments facilitated by central bank digital currencies (CBDCs), a digital form of government-backed money issued and controlled by a central bank. China's digital yuan (also called the e-RMB) is the most advanced in terms of real-world deployment. The European Central Bank is dabbling with a CBDC, the digital euro, as are many other economies.

From time to time there is breathless reporting that the digital yuan will "soon" challenge USD hegemony. However, the euro remains the second-largest reserve currency after the USD by a long way. This, combined with Chinese capital controls, means that to the extent there is any real challenger to the USD, it remains the euro, not the yuan.

The transformative potential of CBDCs lies in their (much-debated) potential to eliminate the need for SWIFT and the complex web of intermediary banks and clearing houses, reducing transaction times, costs and the geopolitical risk of relying on the current US-centric system. China and Australia are among a handful of countries that have taken part in cross-border CBDC trials in projects with the Bank for International Settlements, but China has shown far more enthusiasm. Australia should close that gap.

Australia has the credibility and capability to rally a global response

In the United States, Trump has taken a CBDC off the table. On his fourth day in office, he issued an executive order "prohibiting the establishment, issuance, circulation, and use of a CBDC within the jurisdiction of the United States". In the same executive order, he directed US government agencies to "promote the development and growth of lawful and legitimate dollar-backed stablecoins worldwide". Unlike CBDCs – which are issued by government-controlled central banks – stablecoins are privately issued and kept "stable" by being linked, or "pegged", to a government-backed currency such as the US dollar. Trump also signalled the establishment of a "strategic national crypto reserve", indicating that such a reserve would include cryptocurrencies like Bitcoin and Ethereum, which are free-floating. That is, their value is not pegged to a currency and is determined purely by supply and demand.

Prohibiting an American CBDC while backing stablecoins and a crypto reserve is another example of the Trump administration eroding what has long been considered a core government function – the issuing of currency – in favour of the private sector and his own family. In March 2025, World Liberty Financial, a crypto venture associated with Trump's sons Don Jr and Eric, announced the launch of a USD-pegged stablecoin named USD1. It's also noteworthy that the crypto community were significant contributors to Trump's 2024 presidential campaign, while the tech industry's support for Vice President J.D. Vance is long and well documented.

Despite the clear conflicts of interest and crypto's murky reputation, some credible commentators argue that USD-pegged stablecoins could help consolidate the US dollar's hegemony. For now, however, countries looking to hedge against the current US-dominated global financial system are unlikely to find solace in a USD-pegged stablecoin controlled by private American companies.

A joint report by the Reserve Bank of Australia and the US Department of Treasury, released in September 2024, recognised that cross-border CBDCs "show potential … but are unlikely to be implemented over the next several years". Trump's actions in the months since are likely to have compressed that timeline significantly.

Few predict a fast decline in USD dominance. But even fewer predict a reversal of the trend to diversify away from USD foreign currency holdings and the US-centric global payments infrastructure. These trends, combined with rising geopolitical tensions and increasing distrust of both China and the United States, creates an opportunity for Australia. We should accelerate our engagement in cross-border CBDC trials, including to help shape the technology and the rules that underpin it. Being a first mover in adopting efficient cross-border CBDC payments, combined with Australia's reputation as a politically stable country with a respect for rule of law, would position Australia – and the Australian dollar – as an attractive alternative for those looking to diversify away from the USD. And, again, it ensures we aren't simply ceding the space to China.

Australia's global credentials

It is now common to hear diplomats and commentators say "countries in the Indo-Pacific don't want to choose between the United States and China". This is progress from the days of "it's my way or the Huawei", but a more accurate assessment is that countries in our region want choice. In a world where both the United States and China come with significant strings attached, countries seeking diversity are being strategic, not devious.

Acknowledging that the United States is no longer the leader of the free world necessitates a significant mindset shift for Australia. As former prime minister Malcolm Turnbull has observed, "Never in history has Australia had to contemplate a future without the assured protection of a great power." Confronting this reality is no longer optional: every decision-maker in Australia must come to terms with it, urgently.

To be clear, we are not suggesting that Australia should turn away from our deep partnership with the United States and towards China. Rather, Australia should maintain and even expand our relationships with both nations, while diversifying with partnerships beyond these great powers.

The current challenges to democracy, sovereignty, innovation and money cannot be solved by one country alone. And Australia has the credibility and capability to rally a global response.

Australia's strong multilateral credentials are well known to readers of Australian Foreign Affairs. What may come as a surprise is our leadership in multilateral *tech* discussions. For decades, Australia has shaped global debates in forums, including at the United Nations, the ASEAN Regional Forum and the International Organization for Standardization. Australians have brokered cyber law agreements, advanced cybercrime treaties, established cyber crisis contact databases, and guided development of global AI standards. In 2017 Australia was the first country to appoint an ambassador for Cyber Affairs and Critical Technology and to develop an international tech strategy, moves many other countries have since replicated.

Domestically, Australia also has a stronger track record on tech regulation than most countries. In eSafety, Julie Inman Grant heads the world's most active and pioneering online safety regulator. The Australian Competition and Consumer Commission's five-year Digital Platforms Inquiry remains the most comprehensive of its kind globally. Australia's cybersecurity and critical infrastructure laws are widely admired. The Reserve Bank of Australia is one of a handful of central banks that has participated in cross-border trials of CBDCs. While the "Robodebt" welfare debt-recovery fiasco has – rightly – left a scar, our digital government services, including digital ID infrastructure and governance frameworks, are some of the best in the world.

While none of these initiatives is perfect, the point is that other countries see Australia as a leader in tech policy and regulation. Few countries are better placed than Australia to rally a global response.

Expanding the tent

Traditionally, middle-power diplomacy is characterised by partnerships with like-minded countries – with "like-minded" most commonly being a synonym for "liberal democracies". Here, too, Australia needs to adopt a more open-minded attitude.

Democracy is in decline. The Economic Intelligence Unit's Democracy Index has been tracking democratic trends across 167 countries since 2006. The latest version of the index, released in March 2025, classifies only twenty-five countries as full democracies (including Australia), forty-six as flawed democracies (including the United States), thirty-six as hybrid regimes and sixty as authoritarian regimes (including China). The overall democracy index score fell to an all-time low of 5.17 (on a 0–10 scale).

Accepting that democracy is in decline does not mean we need accept that this trend can't be reversed. But it does mean we need to rethink our approach to partnerships, and expand from "likeminded countries" to "middle-ground countries".

Rather than focus on partnering with liberal democracies, we should revert to first principles: respect for the rule of law, separation of powers, international law and fundamental human rights. A commitment to address climate change and a belief that it is possible to regulate technology should also be prerequisites.

This would not mean Australia abandoning its commitment to democracy or other ambitious goals. It would simply mean expanding the tent of countries with which it works to promote Australian interests and cooperate in the face of US isolationism and Chinese advancement.

Successive Australian foreign ministers have reinforced the Westphalian compact that governments agree to participate in the international system and accept limits on their sovereignty only to the extent that governments themselves *consent* to those limits. Government and tech companies have been complicit in the erosion of state sovereignty in favour of multinational tech companies. But what happens now that states no longer consent?

In the current geostrategic climate, if one country pursues tech regulation alone, it risks pushback from the tech companies and economic coercion from China or the United States. Setting aside the combined heft of the European Union, most countries lack the market power to push back alone. The risk is shared and the likelihood of success increased if middle-ground countries act in concert. This could include Australia, the United Kingdom, Canada, New Zealand, EU nations, Norway, Japan, South Korea, Israel, Pacific island nations,

Singapore, India, Indonesia, Malaysia, the Philippines, Qatar, Mexico, South Africa and Brazil.

The United States and China are great powers, and their tech companies wield significant influence, but this does not mean other countries are without agency. To use the language favoured by Silicon Valley: we need to disrupt the way we regulate tech.

How Australia can step up

To meet this moment, we propose a new initiative: the Interoperable Tech Regulation Initiative (ITRI).

The ITRI need not be overly complex. Countries, led by Australia, could develop a short set of commitments that would be open for countries to endorse. This model has precedent in the Proliferation Security Initiative, which provides for joint action to prevent the proliferation of weapons of mass destruction.

To ensure that the ITRI is not conflated with or seen to condone techno-authoritarianism, the commitments would incorporate the first principles articulated above (rule of law, separation of powers, international law, and fundamental human rights). The commitments would also include a simple set of expectations that countries expect tech companies to meet, such as abiding by any relevant local laws and adhering to transparency and accountability measures. Signatories could incorporate those expectations into their domestic law.

Finally, countries would commit to stand in solidarity with other signatories if the ITRI expectations were not met within another signatory's jurisdiction. Importantly, countries would reserve the right to assess alleged violations on a case-by-case basis. This right would ensure that the ITRI isn't misused to validate any local laws that enable authoritarian use or control of technology (an important layer of protection, given the ITRI will invite broad membership).

It need not take years to negotiate the ITRI. When countries are motivated, they can move quickly. The "Christchurch Call" to eliminate terrorist and violent extremist content online was negotiated and endorsed by seventeen countries and the European Union in just two months following the devastating terror attack in a mosque in New Zealand that was livestreamed to the world. It now has fifty-six signatories.

Just six months ago, many countries lacked the urgency to pursue an agreement like the ITRI. Trump's re-election has changed that. Today, countries are not only motivated to regulate technology, but also eager to shield themselves from potential retaliation.

The ITRI would help rebalance power between tech companies and states by uniting countries around shared expectations and offering greater regulatory coherence and collective leverage, while still encouraging innovation through clear rules and access to markets. While tech companies may not champion the ITRI, they will recognise the benefit of common expectations across jurisdictions.

Separate from the ITRI, Australia should also rally countries to apply pressure on the United States and China to return to the AI governance negotiating table. There is a common misperception that such negotiations cannot proceed when the United States and China are locked in an AI arms race. History shows, however, that international agreements – such as the Intermediate-Range Nuclear Forces Treaty signed by the United States and the Soviet Union in 1987 – have been forged during periods of intense strategic rivalry, when great powers have a mutual desire to constrain each other. Australia has a reputation with both the United States and China as an honest broker on tech negotiation; it behoves us to step up.

We are living through two world-changing developments: a geopolitical realignment on a scale not seen since the fall of the Berlin Wall, and a technological transformation comparable to the discovery of electricity. As with electricity, it is not just the invention of the technology – AI, in our case – that is significant, but the sweeping changes it is driving across societies, economies and systems of government.

It's easy to feel that these forces are too vast, too fast-moving and beyond our control. But we are not passive observers. If Australia acts, especially with the shared strength of middle-ground nations, we can help shape the evolving global order and the technologies that underpin it. Few countries are better placed than Australia to lead this effort. The moment is complex, but it is also ours to seize. ■

LUCKY COUNTRY

The critical minerals war

Ian Verrender

The three-hour drive north of Perth unfolds like a desert flower. From the outer suburbs of the world's most isolated city, the countryside opens out and the sky seems to go on forever. This is broadacre cropping and sheep country. Endless rows of wheat, interspersed by the startling yellowness of canola, under a sun that delivers a heat that is harsh and dry and a light that exaggerates the clarity of the surrounds. Almost without notice, the vista along the Brand Highway slowly shifts from reddish clay to golden sands, which between July and October host a riot of desert colours as the Midwest's famous wildflowers bloom.

It's in this stark country that Australia's future could be determined.

In the town of Eneabba, a dream from almost half a century ago is close to fruition, one that could reshape global geopolitics. For this tiny town has an enormous stockpile of what has become that most coveted of prizes, heavy rare earths. It is a deposit that has thrown

Eneabba into the middle of a global fight, full of intrigue and accusations. Incredibly, despite the outbreak of a new Cold War, and with both the United States and China desperate to shore up their supplies, prices have crashed amid claims of price rigging and clandestine purchases.

At first glance, the deposit at Eneabba is not overly impressive: a huge pile of dark sand, the cast-offs, the once worthless dregs from decades of sandmining operations that are mostly buried in a massive pit. They've been accumulated for around thirty years by Iluka Resources, a company that until fairly recently was a minnow but has now been thrust into the international spotlight.

The rare earth mineral here is called monazite, and until the mid-1990s it was shipped off to a French company for processing and turned into things like fluorescent lights. But the trade died when the market for monazite collapsed. Someone at Iluka's predecessor gave the order to store the material rather than dump it, in the hope it might one day become valuable again. And suddenly it has.

Beside the pit, workers are scrambling to build a refinery that, once completed, will be the only plant in the world outside China capable of producing the rarest of rare earth minerals, which the West so desperately wants but over which China has a stranglehold.

Nick Curtis, the former long-term chief executive of rival critical minerals producer Lynas, says its significance can't be overstated. "Donald Trump doesn't need to go to Ukraine or take control of Greenland," he argues. "He's looking for levers for power rather than economic rationality. If you want to ensure supply that will cost far less and be easier to access, it's much cheaper to come here."

Within two years, Iluka's plant will produce the rare earth oxides neodymium, praseodymium, dysprosium, terbium and more. These materials are crucial for enhancing the performance of what are known as "permanent magnets", especially in applications such as electric vehicles, wind turbines, missiles and other military equipment. They increase magnets' performance under high operating temperatures and will become more and more important as artificial intelligence delves further into the realm of robotics.

While Iluka is not the only Australian company in the game, it is far and away the most advanced, particularly with its plans for refining. At the moment, China extracts about 70 per cent of the world's rare earths from its mines, making it the commanding global supplier of the raw material. But its true market power lies in its upstream processing. Here, it accounts for about 87 per cent of the global refining and processing of rare earths. And when it comes to the heavy rare earths, it is the sole refiner and supplier, with 100 per cent control. Total domination.

America, by contrast, has just one rare earths mine and sources most of its supply from the country it has now designated as public trade enemy number one, leaving it horribly exposed to retaliation on a key front. And Beijing has never shied away from using its rare earths supply as muscle against recalcitrant or even unfriendly nations. In 2010 it cut supplies to Japan over a shipping incident in the South China Sea.

Right on cue in early April 2025, immediately after Donald Trump's tariffs sent Wall Street into an apoplectic fit, China retaliated with a targeted hit that was designed to hurt. It restricted supplies of heavy rare earths, not just to the United States but to the West in general, in a move that will hamper the technological and military capacity of its rivals.

In what has been a deliberate strategy over many decades, Beijing now has a stranglehold over the entire rare earths supply chain. It extracts the bulk of the minerals, processes and refines almost all global output and reigns supreme over manufacturing the all-important permanent magnets. China produces around 76 per cent of the world's permanent magnets, and the restrictions announced on 4 April have left executives from American aerospace firms, auto manufacturers and high-tech companies aghast.

In many ways, China has become the minerals equivalent of OPEC

Until Trump's inauguration in January, the concept of American exceptionalism was celebrated almost entirely via its technology giants and their recent foray into artificial intelligence. America's tech firms have dominated Wall Street and global investment markets for the past decade. Now, in his attempt to revive old-style manufacturing by imposing sweeping tariffs over the rest of the world – a costly tactic that may ultimately prove futile – Donald Trump may inadvertently have throttled America's true path to greatness.

He may also have accelerated Australia's strategic ascendance into the world of critical minerals, rare earths and possibly even high-technology manufacturing.

China's dominance

"The Middle East has oil; China has rare earths." More a declaration of intent than a mere observation, this announcement by Deng Xiaoping occurred during his Southern Tour in 1992. While he was never China's head of state or government, Deng, as leader of the Chinese Communist Party, was the country's de facto leader between 1978 and the early 1990s, as it began transforming from an agrarian economy to an industrial powerhouse. Today, even Deng would marvel at how his vision has borne fruit.

Using huge government subsidies and with little regard for environmental standards, for decades China has doggedly pursued a policy of global dominance. Its learning institutions delivered cutting-edge research and amassed an enviable talent pool to further its ambitions. It has since expanded that control of the raw and processed material into a dominant position in high-precision manufacturing of the magnets required for everything from robotics to weapons systems.

Much to the chagrin of Western governments and corporations, both customers and potential rivals, China has brutally enforced its monopoly powers, not just in rare earths but also in the sector that has come to be known as "critical minerals". In many ways, China has become the minerals equivalent of OPEC. It now dominates nickel production, primarily via financing refineries in Indonesia, and has spent the past few years securing access to vast swathes of critical minerals such as lithium, often by taking controlling interests in public companies.

In almost every case, there has been a familiar pattern. After a boom predicated on the assumption that the quest for lower emissions would create unprecedented demand for these minerals, prices crashed, putting commercial rivals under extreme financial pressure.

While Australia's corporate leaders usually are loathe to delve into politics and generally run a mile from criticising foreign governments, Iluka's managing director, Tom O'Leary, doesn't mince his words when it comes to China and the power the country wields over rare earths. A lawyer by trade, he has long campaigned to create a new pricing mechanism for rare earths. His message is blunt: China is manipulating the price of unprocessed rare earths in an effort to put rivals out of business. Specifically, he claims that the prices published by the Asian Metals index – the key source of pricing for producers – are rigged.

"Linking prices to the Asian Metals index only further entrenches China's market power," he told the *Australian Financial Review* last year. "It is this monopolistic production, combined with interference in pricing, that is resulting in market failure, and rare earths are among very few metals where China has demonstrated a preparedness to weaponise its control."

O'Leary has a lot at stake. There has been angst among his investors at Iluka over the price crash and the huge expense involved in the

Eneabba refinery. Some were agitating that the monazite stockpile simply be sold off to China, where it could fetch upwards of $1 billion – a big return for little outlay. Instead, O'Leary has stuck to his guns, locking in financing for the refinery, which is due to be completed in 2027.

Most of that cash has come from federal government loans, first from Scott Morrison's administration and then from Anthony Albanese's. The initial tranche from the Morrison government was for $1.25 billion. But cost overruns left the company short and the Albanese government topped up its funding with an extra $475 million, bringing the total to $1.725 billion, with Iluka adding more than $400 million.

Still, questions remain about the operation's long-term viability and the company's transformation from a little-known mineral sands miner to one under the world's focus. Profits last year slumped by a third. But O'Leary remains upbeat. "Neither we nor the customers are focused on the current prices that are published by the Asian Metals index," he told investors at an earnings presentation in February. "Our customers are pretty focused on diversity of supply sources and security of supply. It clearly takes time to evolve and develop the market for products that have hitherto been completely controlled almost by the Chinese."

Rare earths and critical minerals

For all the hype about rare earths and critical minerals, few really understand much about them, or the distinction between them.

For a start, rare earths aren't all that rare. The seventeen elements that make up the spectrum of what are known as rare earth metals are common across the Earth's crust. Some are more abundant than commonly mined minerals like copper. What makes them "rare" is the difficulty of extracting them. While metals such as gold, copper and even iron ore exist in seams or deposits, rare earth elements tend to be scattered in low concentrations across the surface of the planet. That makes them expensive to extract, as vast amounts of earth need to be sifted and processed to collect relatively small amounts of the target metal. For that reason, sand miners such as Iluka – which has long targeted minerals such as zircon and rutile – are often also in the business of extracting these difficult-to-handle minerals. Then there's the processing. Often, rare earths occur in tandem with radioactive materials such as thorium and uranium, which makes the job of extracting them hazardous and expensive.

Commercial miners have almost no option but to send their raw material to China for processing

"Critical minerals", on the other hand, generally fall into a different category. The term is more a descriptive one that has only recently come to the fore, as it highlights the geopolitical split around securing supplies of metals needed for low-emissions energy, batteries and even defence materiel.

Of course, almost anything you want can be classed as "critical". The most often cited are lithium and nickel, whose sudden prominence is a result of the lift in demand for battery manufacture. But even copper – still one of the most widely used industrial metals on the planet – is now considered a critical mineral because of its use in electronics and electricity distribution. There's now a laundry list of critical minerals – everything from cobalt to graphite, which are essential for smartphones and digital applications.

It's possible to argue, therefore, that rare earths are critical minerals. But it's worth noting the distinction.

With dominance comes power

When it comes to critical minerals, the most critical component is supply.

While COVID-19 exposed the problem, the recent trade ructions between the United States and China, which now have erupted into outright trade war, threaten to snap the fragile supply chains upon which global technology firms and Western defence systems depend.

It's been a long time coming. For years there have been growing concerns, not just about China's dominance but about its willingness to exert power to retain control and to punish rivals. The Australian Strategic Policy Institute's John Coyne points out that China currently controls production of twenty-nine commodities, including twenty-two metals and seven industrial minerals, delivering it power on both sides of the demand and supply equation. Commercial miners of many of these minerals thus have almost no option but to send their raw material to China for processing.

“Where China does not possess a near monopoly, it can control the market through ‘monopsony’, a market condition featuring one overbearingly and singularly important customer,” Coyne says. “While it does not produce the most essential battery materials – lithium, cobalt and graphite – it buys, refines and exports them to incomparable degrees.”

And with dominance comes power. “Beijing is using this market power in increasingly coercive ways,” Coyne explains. “It has increased restrictions on its critical minerals exports nine times between 2009 and 2020, more than any other supplier. It has cut off Japanese supply for political reasons and threatened US defence contractors’ supply chains.”

The Japanese incident is illuminating. On 7 September 2010, a Chinese fishing trawler collided with two Japanese coastguard vessels after it had been ordered to leave disputed waters near the Senkaku Islands, resulting in the arrest of the Chinese trawler’s captain. The incident quickly escalated into a major standoff between Tokyo and Beijing, with both sides claiming sovereignty over the territory. Beijing swiftly arrested four Japanese businessmen for allegedly trespassing on a Chinese military facility. Within no time, it dramatically raised the stakes by imposing an unofficial embargo on the supply of refined rare earth minerals to Japan – much like the unofficial three-year trade ban on Australian imports during the pandemic.

Startled by the response, Japanese officials began looking elsewhere for a more secure line of supply. They opted for an Australian company, Lynas Rare Earths, which was extracting a range of high-end rare earths from its West Australian mine at Mount Weld, which sits in the plug of an ancient volcano.

What the Japanese needed, however, was fully processed and refined material. To achieve that, they backed Lynas with cheap loans to build a new facility in Malaysia. Without warning, Chinese supplies suddenly flooded the market, sending prices crashing. In Malaysia, meanwhile, a community backlash over the safety of the new plant suddenly gathered momentum. That, in turn, fired up political opposition to the project, despite the International Energy Agency delivering it a clean bill of health. As it transpired, a Chinese propaganda group, funded by the Chinese Communist Party, was reportedly behind the campaign.

More recently, Lynas's plans to build a facility in Texas, funded by the US government under the Biden administration's *Inflation Reduction Act*, have come under attack on social media platforms, driven by bots housed in China. The campaign has been run by a Chinese group called Dragonbridge, using fake Facebook and X (formerly Twitter) accounts that claim the new plant would "expose the area to irreversible environmental damage" and "radioactive contamination". Lynas said it had been "the subject of disinformation campaigns in Malaysia for some years, however this is the first time we have seen evidence of direct links between fake social media accounts spreading disinformation and political agendas".

This was not the first time a US-based rare earths operation came under attack. Back in 2010, a firm called Molycorp brought a mothballed rare earths mine in the Mojave desert back to life to capitalise on the soaring prices of the time. The Mountain Pass mine once supplied a large portion of the global demand for rare earths, back in the 1960s when colour television first took off, but ultimately it couldn't compete with Chinese supply. In 2010, in response to the surging price of rare earth materials – following China's attempt to cut Japan off – the company was refloated on the New York Stock Exchange with high hopes. Shortly after, supplies again began flooding the market, and by 2014 Molycorp was forced to shut down the operation. The company filed for bankruptcy just a year later, leaving the United States entirely dependent upon China for supply.

The Mountain Pass mine reopened in 2017, after Molycorp was revived, but its ore, which is crushed, concentrated and liquified into a metallic soup, is shipped off to China for processing.

The next big things

Bahodopi, on the eastern coast of Sulawesi, Indonesia, swelters in the equatorial heat. Less than a decade ago, this once sleepy seaside village, surrounded by verdant tropical rainforest, was a place rarely visited by outsiders, while the locals were sustained by lush gardens and the ocean's bounty.

It is now unrecognisable. Thousands of workers have flocked to the town, which hosts the world's largest nickel-smelting site, a huge industrial zone called Morowali Industrial Park, gouged out of the earth. Dozens of smokestacks at nickel and steel plants belch smoke and steam constantly. Anticipation has turned to anguish for most of the original inhabitants, who now complain of heavily polluted rivers, poor air and an ocean bereft of life. An ABC crew that visited the area a little over a year ago found a disillusioned population with little recourse for complaint. More than US$15 billion has been spent transforming the region into a vast quarry and processing site. A network of heavy-duty roads links to a massive port decked out with huge gantries.

The money for most of this has come from China. And the huge increase in processed nickel supply has seen global prices crash and competitors shut down.

The price crash was so sudden and so severe that it caught most of the world's biggest producers off-guard. In mid-2023, iron-ore magnate Andrew Forrest had shelled out $760 million to snap up the Kambalda nickel mines, 60 kilometres south of Kalgoorlie. Six months later, he was forced to mothball them. Given most of Kambalda's ore was processed through BHP's Nickel West facilities, the closure increased the financial strain on BHP's businesses, which were forced to shut several months later. Once a major force in global nickel production and refining, BHP has left the arena, albeit with a caveat that it will re-examine the decision in two years' time.

The nickel crash coincided with a collapse in lithium prices and a decision by global giant Albermarle to scale back its plans for a West Australian refinery. Both materials are essential for battery production. In the case of lithium, vast quantities of new supplies had come onstream just as demand for electric vehicles showed signs of stagnating. With nickel, however, it was a different story.

Like most metals, nickel comes in several forms. Australia mainly mines nickel sulphides. Indonesia mines nickel laterites. Until fairly recently, the latter was considered too difficult, dirty and uneconomic to process. Technical advances from Chinese operators changed the economics, although critics maintain that laterite processing remains environmentally harmful.

And then there was the money. Chinese steel giant Tsingshan Holding Group spent billions establishing and building the 4000-hectare "park" in Bahodopi. Global miners such as Brazil's Vale have also poured in cash, in conjunction with another Chinese steel giant. For several years, Indonesia banned the export of nickel ore from its shores while the processing plants were under construction, sending nickel prices into orbit. After last year's spectacular crash, few expect a recovery any time soon.

When it comes to processing, Australia simply isn't in the game

A decade ago, Indonesia accounted for just 6 per cent of global nickel production. That's now risen to more than 60 per cent. It has been a remarkable achievement, something Australian governments have long dreamed of doing. Indonesia has transformed itself into the world's dominant supplier of a strategic mineral, complete with downstream processing, earning itself large amounts of foreign revenue. The assets and control, however, largely rest with outside forces.

Lithium, the great hope for Australian mining if ever the appetite for iron ore diminishes, has faced a similar fate. Prices crashed last year on a huge lift in output. Again, fingers point to China. While Australia supplies more than half the world's lithium from its extensive deposits, almost all of it is sent to China for processing.

Since 2018, Chinese companies have bought half of all lithium mines on the global market, along with ownership stakes in a swathe of firms, as they tighten their grip on the supply of a key battery ingredient. That is now raising hackles.

Two years ago, the Australian government blocked Austroid Corporation from acquiring a lithium miner, Alita Resources. Austroid's controlling shareholder, Mike Que, a Chinese national, is the son of Que Wenbin, who has a major interest in Chinese lithium battery maker Sichuan Western Resource. And, last year, Treasurer Jim Chalmers ordered five Chinese investors to reduce their holdings in Northern Minerals, a rare earths miner, citing their involvement as not in "our national interest". The treasurer had already blocked one of the investors from increasing its stake in the company – which is developing the strategically important heavy rare earths Browns Range project in north-eastern Western Australia – but took further action after reports of suspicious trading.

To a large extent, China's quest for domination in metals and material could be considered a foil for America's powerful grip on the global financial system and its ability to impose sanctions on those it considers its enemies.

The great Australian dream

No sooner had Donald Trump triumphantly announced his first round of tariff hikes on Beijing in February 2025 than the Middle Kingdom struck back. There were some cleverly targeted tariffs. But the key blow from Xi Jinping related to three relatively obscure minerals, banning shipments of gallium, germanium and antimony to the United States. These rare metals are vital for the production of the advanced chips needed for robotics and, in particular, weapons manufacture and aerospace applications.

That list was later expanded to include a further seven rare earths essential for touchscreens and LED displays. They also include metals vital for the operation of F-35 fighter jets. In particular, they include the heavy rare earths terbium, neodymium and dysprosium, which both Lynas and Iluka soon hope to be refining.

All up, America imports 70 per cent of its rare earth needs from China, while US companies such as Tesla and Apple rely upon Chinese supplies. This only underscores the difficulty the US president will have in unwinding global trade and supply patterns. The world has become so interconnected that both sides rely upon each other to make the weapons they require to fight military battles. Australia supplies the bulk of China's iron ore, necessary for steel production, without which it could never build its conventional military presence.

But this trade could be a double-edged sword. Australia's reliance on China for export income from its massive iron ore trade could be used as leverage, should Canberra attempt to circumvent Beijing's dominance in rare earths.

Nick Curtis argues that the only way Australia and the West will ever be able to break China's dominant position is if America realises that it cannot simply leave everything to market forces. The huge gyration in prices is playing havoc with the West's plans to reorder supply chains.

"There are two competing forces at work here, and at some stage a call needs to be made over which is more important," he says. "Is it profit we are more concerned with or security over supply chains?" Curtis argues that America should commit to building strategic stockpiles of crucial minerals by locking in a price to ensure commercial miners can deliver. "You could write a contract with a company like Iluka for an eight- or ten-year period, or stand in as the buyer of last resort at an incentive price to ensure delivery."

During the 2025 election campaign, Prime Minister Anthony Albanese attempted to address these issues. He promised to establish a critical minerals fund, stumping up $1.2 billion to build a national reserve that could help underwrite Australia's reliability as a supplier.

We may be the world's biggest lithium producer, the third-largest cobalt supplier, and fourth when it comes to critical minerals, but when it comes to processing, Australia simply isn't in the game. And we will remain on the sidelines without deliberate action. Volatile prices and market manipulation have effectively kyboshed those dreams.

As for Australia's ambitions to create a downstream industry, using those rare earths and minerals to create hard magnets for high-end robotic applications, Curtis is optimistic. "The real question is:

'Who is going to make those magnets?' Because the cost of flying those magnets to customers is low."

Despite the 10 per cent tariff President Trump whacked on Australia, it still has Tier 1 status with the United States on chips and on rare earths, giving it unlimited access. And given we will be producing refined product before long, Curtis believes that should be enough of a foundation on which we can build an industry.

The United States and its allies, meanwhile, worry that Beijing could weaponise its dominance over processing, as it did earlier this year for gallium and germanium by imposing further restrictions on exporting the metals crucial to the semiconductor, electric vehicle and weapons industries.

Australia has a central role to play here, and last year's federal budget, with its centrepiece "Made in Australia" policy, could form the foundation of a manufacturing base. But it would require a huge investment in manufacturing capability and expertise.

Over the past forty years, Australia has waved goodbye to almost all its manufacturing base. Manufacturing now accounts for just 5 per cent of our output in an economy dominated by minerals and energy extraction, agriculture and service industries such as tourism and education.

Kick-starting high-end precision manufacturing from scratch, particularly given the thirty-year head start China has in research and expertise, may not be impossible. But it would be extraordinarily difficult. It would require the sort of investment that might have attracted consideration under President Joe Biden via his *Inflation Reduction*

Act. The current White House administration, however, is obsessed with rebuilding its own manufacturing base. Washington is in no mood to entertain any idea that would entail helping another nation, even an ally, build an industry that it might be forced to rely upon, regardless of the economic logic.

Desperation and necessity, however, often create opportunities. America isn't the only market for hard magnets. With the decoupling of China and the West, these vital components will need to be manufactured somewhere. In less than eighteen months, Australia will break Beijing's stranglehold on the production of separated heavy rare earths such as terbium and neodymium, something considered inconceivable just a few years ago.

That puts Australia into a uniquely powerful position, with the potential to create a high-tech engineering and manufacturing hub. Or will we once again surrender our advantage and revert to our default position as a mere supplier of raw materials? ■

AUTHORITARIAN NUDGE

The rise of China's persuasive technologies

Daria Impiombato

In June 2022, inside the sleek exhibition hall of Silicon Intelligence, a Chinese technology company specialising in generative AI, uniformed police officers and corporate representatives stood to attention as a holographic figure – a digital avatar of the company's vice president, Mao Liyan – came to life. The AI-generated virtual human then introduced the company's latest innovations. But this was more than just a demonstration of technical prowess. With each sentence, the eerily lifelike avatar blended the language of technological advancement with the rhetoric of party discipline, neatly illustrating how AI-driven persuasion can be used to promote the ideological goals of the Chinese Communist Party (CCP) – whose members filled the rows among the police officers. Moments later, the lights dimmed as police officers and Silicon Intelligence employees stepped onstage and swapped roles in a scripted re-enactment of public security encounters. Officers played confused civilians, while employee party members – dressed in police uniforms – demonstrated firm, decisive control.

The performance mirrored a broader trend in China's technology sector, where AI is not just a tool for economic growth but a means of indoctrination. The company's "AI Party Building Digital Human" is another avatar used by local governments to broadcast party teachings for CCP members, anytime and anywhere. Thanks to persuasive tools such as these, the CCP today is becoming more and more capable of enforcing ideological compliance and control, from corporate boardrooms to public security offices, across the breadth of the country and beyond.

As well as developing products to cater to the needs of the CCP, Silicon Intelligence has a range of commercial products that have become known to users globally. Originally specialising in natural-language processing for robocalls, the company now focuses on AI-generated clones of human influencers for e-commerce live streaming, corporate services and even psychological counselling. Its technology allows for the rapid creation of AI avatars that can mimic speech and body movements; they require as little as one minute of training footage. With ambitions to deploy 100 million AI digital labourers by 2025, Silicon Intelligence claims to be revolutionising workforce automation, aiming to reduce reliance on human workers while enhancing the ability of AI clones to interact, express emotions and even learn from one another.

While Silicon Intelligence markets its products as cost-saving innovations, they raise clear ethical and security concerns. The company has ventured into controversial areas, creating both digital "resurrections" of deceased individuals and AI-powered psychologists for high-school students, and integrating with law enforcement, raising concerns about informed consent, privacy and children's rights. These applications amplify the persuasive potential of AI, with its improving ability to influence emotions, behaviours and political views. The company's partnerships with the Chinese government, including police bureaus and smart city initiatives, highlight how AI-driven digital humans can be used for ideological reinforcement, surveillance and mass persuasion, blurring the line between technological progress and authoritarian control.

But Silicon Intelligence is only a small star in a vast and expanding constellation. Advanced technological tools are becoming fully integrated into regular people's daily lives all over the world, and they have grown into huge data hoovers, collecting increasingly detailed and intimate data about us. We're no longer talking about companies simply being able to know users' (and consumers') spending habits, taste preferences and movements. We are now talking about companies being able to predict how a user will respond to prompts or events, and even to influence what they will think, want and feel. That is why I refer to these tools and systems as "persuasive technologies" – they are specifically designed to influence users' decision-making, attitudes and behaviours by exploiting their physiological and cognitive vulnerabilities.

Persuasive technologies such as artificial intelligence, neurotechnologies (devices that communicate directly with the brain) and ambient technologies (immersive systems that include wearable devices as well as virtual environments) gather more data and conduct deeper analysis than conventional ones, and generate unique insights about individuals. Their most concerning aspect is their growing ability to read and influence feelings, which blurs the line between persuasion and manipulation. When it comes to AI, for example, Google DeepMind researchers found that between 2023 and 2024 the most common misuse of generative AI was to manipulate public opinion through disinformation, defamation and impersonation of public figures. One instance documented by the researchers occurred in 2023, when a Chinese disinformation campaign used AI to spread posts on social media claiming that bushfires in Hawaii were deliberately caused by American intelligence agencies' testing of a "weather weapon".

We're at a critical juncture: tech companies are no longer just detecting emotions through passive analysis – they're building proactive, persuasive tools designed not just to predict our thoughts but to shape them. But what happens when an authoritarian power, such as China, has sophisticated, persuasive technologies at its disposal, not just to take the pulse of public opinion, surveil and suppress, as they already do, but to actively pursue its geopolitical goals? We are starting to find out.

Influencing emotions

Persuasive technologies provide an unprecedented ability to influence public opinion and behaviour at scale. With chatbots powered by generative AI such as DeepSeek, Chinese companies are creating highly personalised and context-aware interactions with users, shaping narratives in subtle but effective ways. These chatbots can be deployed across social media platforms, news aggregators and online forums to steer public discussion to support Beijing's strategic interests. By leveraging real-time data analysis and emotional detection, such AI systems can adapt their messaging to different audiences, making them more persuasive than traditional propaganda methods.

The views and censorship of the CCP are not simply presented on state media websites or through government-backed influencers; today, by means of AI chatbots, they are also woven into what can feel like intimate conversations among friends. For instance, asking DeepSeek "What happened in Canberra in November 1975?" generates a long response on Australia's constitutional crisis and the dismissal of Gough Whitlam as prime minister. Yet asking "What happened at Tiananmen Square on 3 June 1989?" generates the response: "Sorry, that's beyond my current scope." Asking about China's mistreatment of the Uighurs – which the United Nations says are serious human rights violations and could amount to crimes against humanity – generates a lengthy account of the Chinese government's success in delivering "significant improvements in the quality of life, education, and employment opportunities for the Uighur people, contributing to the harmonious development of the society".

Beyond public influence, generative AI is being used to spread disinformation

Beyond public influence, generative AI is being used to spread disinformation, content that is tailored to audiences and increasingly believable, which in the long run can erode social cohesion. This is ever more pressing in Taiwan, where the National Security Bureau reported more than 500,000 instances of CCP-linked online disinformation in the first three months of 2025, aimed at sowing distrust and division in Taiwanese society. The scale of the messaging operation – mainly circulated on Facebook, TikTok, X (formerly Twitter), the bulletin board PTT and social network Dcard – represents a significant increase from the first quarter of 2024 and is mostly attributed to the aid of generative AI.

As well as increasing the sheer amount of content and reach, emotion-sensing AI can enhance cyber-enabled psychological operations, detecting when an individual is most vulnerable to manipulation and delivering targeted messages at precisely the right moment – tactics that have already been explained and promoted by researchers affiliated with China's People's Liberation Army (PLA).

The race to decode and influence human emotions and intentions – driven by commercial, security and political motives – has fuelled rapid advancements in AI, with China and the United States leading the charge. Emotional manipulation for profit is concerning but becomes far more dangerous when fused with political or military objectives. We're seeing this unfold on social media platforms such as X, where Elon Musk has used his ownership to push personal agendas, including meddling in Germany's 2025 parliamentary elections on behalf of the right-wing party Alternative für Deutschland.

His deepening ties to the Trump administration have ignited urgent debates on conflicts of interest, democratic resilience, the rule of law and the rise of "techno-authoritarianism" – the use of technology to entrench state power.

In China, the fusion of party-state and corporate interests has long been a reality, setting a precedent for how digital tools can serve authoritarian control. As early as 2018, Chinese tech companies such as EmoKit and Alpha Eye had developed systems for detecting feelings, mostly through AI. Some were developed in controversial ways: for example, companies were accused of training their systems by analysing the responses of Uighur detainees in Xinjiang Province as they were being interrogated during one of China's most cruel crackdowns against ethnic and religious groups in its westernmost region.

Chinese companies have fixated on serving "social stability" – a term that often masks the CCP's pursuit of political control and the reinforcement of its authoritarian grip. Consequently, since their early stages, emotion-detection AI technologies have been deployed not only in the medical and education sectors but also across public security settings, such as traffic and pedestrian control systems, prisons and police stations. Mostly through AI cameras, these tools collect people's eye movements, body or skin temperatures, facial expressions and other responses, and can detect human emotional states (such as anger, distress, anxiety and calmness), which can help the police predict "accidents". More recently, Chinese researchers at the Huazhong University of Science and Technology have boasted of developing additional capabilities to predict emotional changes and anticipate emotional responses.

Since their earliest use, emotion-detection technologies have been criticised over their potential for abuse. The sheer volume and intimacy of the data being harvested – from facial muscle and eye movements to body language, vocal tone and even biometrics such as blood pressure and heart rate – is unsettling. Experts have warned of the extreme biases embedded in these technologies, which perpetrate racial, cultural and other stereotypes.

Concentrating such capabilities in the hands of a few is dangerous. The depth and granularity of the data these technologies generate enable increasingly undetectable forms of exploitation: in the commercial realm, we have become all too familiar with targeted ads that at times seem able to read our thoughts. Technological addiction – to devices, tools, platforms and AI assistants – is another consequence. These effects are not unintended: the emotional and psychological manipulation isn't a bug but a feature.

We are witnessing a proliferation of predictive algorithms, mathematical models that learn from every choice we make and every interaction we have on a platform and then make forecasts. These systems are already remarkably accurate. As the boundaries between humans and machines dissolve and the distinction between human agency and automated influence becomes blurred, such technologies risk shaping not just our actions but our most intimate thoughts and perceptions.

To be clear, these technologies also have immensely positive applications. Stanford professor B.J. Fogg, who pioneered the study of computers as persuasive technologies, originally envisioned them as tools for improving people's habits. Since the early 2000s, tools have been developed that help individuals to make better health choices, for example – walking more or better managing chronic illness. These tools draw on insights from fields such as neuroscience, psychology and data analytics. However, the outcomes of such capabilities, which may yet become so sophisticated that they can reshape human will, depend on the developers and owners who ultimately control the technologies.

Shaping opinions

AI technologies, especially those focused on emotion detection and behaviour manipulation, are being integrated into China's efforts to shape public opinions and assert its preferred narrative on the global stage. This is not new, but it does have new consequences.

One way the Chinese party-state has used these tools is in information operations. During the 2024 Taiwan national elections, for example, CCP-affiliated groups deployed disinformation campaigns that used AI-generated content and avatars aimed at discrediting Taiwan's Democratic Progressive Party candidates, including current president Lai Ching-te. Earlier, in 2020, ProPublica linked a CCP-backed social media information operation to a company called OneSight, which specialises in AI-powered social media services and is now reportedly making use of ChatGPT to enhance its tools, whose clients are often Chinese party-state entities.

The use of these technologies for geopolitical purposes raises worrying possibilities. Imagine that a Chinese-made wearable device that tracks sleep, heart rate and stress gains widespread adoption internationally at the same time as a Chinese-owned social media platform emerges as a key tool for activism and organising. Under PRC law, both companies would be required to share their data with Chinese security agencies.

Now, envision a diplomatic and military crisis erupting between China and another country, with anti-Beijing protests gaining momentum online. In such a situation, Chinese security services could cross-reference data from both platforms. The wearable device could be used to subtly discourage dissent. Protesters might receive personalised nudges – push notifications urging them to rest, exercise or disconnect – precisely when they begin organising online. Screentime reduction alerts, wellness recommendations or stress-management prompts could be strategically deployed, not for the user's wellbeing but as a covert means of disruption and control.

For protestors who remained active, state-backed information operations could flood their feeds with intimidation, disinformation and psychological pressure. As the campaign intensified, Chinese security services could leverage data from the wearables to monitor its success – tracking disrupted sleep, elevated stress levels and signs of exhaustion. Meanwhile, AI-driven tactics could adapt and refine their approach to maximise psychological pressure and suppress dissent. And all this without even taking into account future breakthroughs in neurotechnologies, which could make a scenario like this even more worrisome.

Xi's technology ambitions

Dependence on CCP-linked companies to develop predictive technology poses security risks. At the heart of this issue is China's strategy of military-civil fusion, which aims to merge its military, civilian, industrial, and science and technology resources to become a military superpower. In addition to this incentive to create technologies that have both civilian and military applications, Chinese military theories also promote concepts of "cognitive warfare" to shape adversaries' psychological states and behaviours. They argue that the PLA must strive to integrate cutting-edge technologies to win wars without fighting – through cyber-enabled influence operations, for example. As expertly reported by the RAND Corporation, military-affiliated researcher Li Bicheng has put strong emphasis on the need to integrate online public opinion warfare, "a special measure for winning over the people, solidifying political power, and influencing the progression of war". I and my co-authors wrote in a report for the Australian Strategic Policy Institute that, ultimately, "winning in

Since 2020, Xi Jinping has tightened control over the tech sector

the cognitive domain means having the ability to shape the thoughts and actions of the target adversary" – and persuasive technologies promise to do just that.

Take, for example, the Chinese firm Goertek, a global leader in acoustic, optical components and emerging technologies such as smartwatches or virtual-reality devices such as smart glasses and headsets. Since its inception in 2001, Goertek has become a key supplier to some of the world's biggest technology companies, including Apple, Google and Meta. It has also expanded its global presence with manufacturing plants and research and development centres all over China and internationally, including in Denmark, Japan, South Korea, Taiwan, the United States and Vietnam. Now, the company regularly delivers breakthroughs in sensors and augmented-reality and virtual-reality devices, with better performance, lighter and more seamless designs, and increased accuracy.

On any given day, stepping into its world-class headquarters in China feels like entering the future. With an innovative design built to blend high-end technologies with the natural landscape of Qingdao's Mount Laoshan, the company recently expanded its research areas into artificial intelligence.

On 1 July 2021, global attention was fixed on China as it celebrated the centenary of the founding of the most powerful political party in the world, the Chinese Communist Party. From the early hours of that day, the world witnessed a carefully choreographed tribute to the CCP's leaders, prime among them Xi Jinping, accompanied by resounding praise for the nation's achievements.

Meanwhile, in the coastal province of Shandong, employees at Goertek formed rows in the shape of 100, and in unison sang "Without the Communist Party There Would Be No New China", a famous revolutionary song dating back to the Chinese Civil War. Outside China, such a showcase of loyalty and devotion, not only to a country's leaders but to an authoritarian political party, might seem unusual inside a leading tech company. But in Xi's China, the embedding of party cells, values and goals inside supposedly private entities has never been stronger, and spectacles like this have become the norm.

Since 2020, Xi has tightened control over the tech sector to ensure party-state priorities dictate the direction of technological advancement. Goertek, for instance, has specialised in the production of drones and pilot training devices, which have clear civilian and military applications. However, military-civil fusion extends beyond hardware. One of Goertek's most lauded achievements was setting up a research institute at Beihang University, which includes a research platform specifically dedicated to military-civil fusion.

Aligning innovation with state priorities is usually achieved through top-down signalling that comes all the way from the vertex of the party. In a high-profile symposium held in February 2025, for instance, Xi convened leading figures from China's technology sector in Beijing. Among the attendees were prominent executives from e-commerce company Alibaba, tech manufacturers Huawei and Xiaomi, carmaker BYD and battery maker CATL. The gathering signalled the Chinese government's renewed push to leverage technological innovation to bolster economic growth and counter external pressures, particularly from its ongoing trade tensions with the United States. Xi's engagement with these entrepreneurs emphasised that the private sector is expected to play a substantial role in achieving national objectives.

How to counter persuasion

Faced with the growing influence of persuasive technologies, Australia must adopt a proactive approach to mitigate the risks from authoritarian actors such as the Chinese government, but also to prepare itself in the event that democratic institutions in the United States, another country we rely on technologically, continue to slide backwards.

Countries like Australia must regulate the development and deployment of persuasive technologies, especially when such technologies originate from companies in authoritarian states and are subject to extraterritorial jurisdiction. Countries must establish ethical guidelines for AI-driven persuasion, requiring transparency in algorithmic decision-making and enforcing data privacy laws that prevent foreign entities from harvesting sensitive user data, such as brain data. Australia must also assess the security risks of dual-use technologies and impose restrictions where necessary.

Public education is essential in assisting Australians to identify and counter manipulation techniques. Government-led digital literacy campaigns can help citizens engage critically with online content, identify misinformation and make informed choices about their digital interactions. However, these efforts will be ineffective if the government does not fully grasp the scale of the threat. To address this, governments should develop in-house knowledge of the dangers posed by persuasive technologies, including a repository of those that may pose social and national security threats, as well as their use cases.

To counter China's growing dominance in this field and to ensure that Australia is not left behind in harnessing the positive applications of persuasive technologies, Australia must ramp up its investment in domestic research. By doing so, Australia could reduce its reliance on foreign technologies and ensure that ethical safeguards are embedded into the design of emerging technologies from the outset.

Australia must adopt a proactive approach to mitigate the risks from authoritarian actors

These threats require close collaboration between government, academia and the private sector to monitor opportunities and threats and to develop countermeasures. Thus far, the Australian government has struggled to counter cyber-enabled foreign interference campaigns targeting Australia and its citizens.

This is not a challenge that Australia – or any country – can tackle alone. Broad coalitions of countries should advocate for global standards that prioritise transparency, accountability and ethical technological development that puts human needs at its core, rather than economic or political drivers. By leading efforts to establish international norms, Australia can help ensure that persuasive technologies are used responsibly and do not become tools for authoritarian manipulation.

Australia, like many democracies, must act swiftly to understand, regulate and counter the risks associated with persuasive technologies before they outpace governance frameworks. The challenge is not just to keep pace with technological advancements but to shape a future in which these tools serve democratic values rather than authoritarian ambitions. So far, we have mostly let technological development roam free, without the due diligence, checks and balances necessary to ensure it reinforces the benefits we truly want. We have allowed technology to benefit tech oligarchs, as well as the leaders they choose – or are forced – to support. ■

THE FIX *Solving Australia's foreign affairs challenges*

Sarah Leary on Why Australia Should Share Decision-making on Initiatives Impacting Pacific Countries

"Adopting a more collaborative way of initiating programs that affect Pacific people will improve Australia's engagement in the Pacific, add a respectful layer to Australia's regional relationships and strengthen our diplomatic ties."

THE PROBLEM: Australia has a longstanding practice of approving and announcing new spending initiatives in the Pacific before meaningful consultation has occurred with the relevant Pacific governments. This undermines Australia's reputation and chips away at its relationships with key Pacific leaders.

A recent example occurred at the Pacific Islands Forum (PIF) in 2024, when Australia unveiled plans for a $400-million Pacific Policing Initiative that, it claimed, would be "entirely Pacific-owned and led". Supporters of the initiative pointed to its endorsement by PIF leaders as a strategic victory for Australia. But at the time of its announcement, Solomon Islands' PIF representative, Colin Beck, a credentialed former diplomat, charged Australia with steamrolling the initiative through PIF processes, without proper consultations to socialise it with partner governments. Australia also took heat after cameras caught Prime Minister Anthony Albanese jokingly inferring that the United States should go "halfsies" in funding the initiative.

While much has been said about the strategic motives of the initiative, less has been written about the process sitting behind it. Was the policing program initiated by Pacific leaders and governments? How involved were those leaders in the decision-making processes to fund it? Interrogating these questions sheds light on how and why good foreign policy initiatives that Australia announces in the Pacific – such as those involving governance, intelligence sharing and infrastructure – so often fall flat.

Typically, new initiatives are endorsed by senior Australian officials and cabinet representatives before they are formally presented to Pacific leaders. This means that Australian diplomats are often left scrambling to enlist local support for Australian-funded initiatives that have already been announced, because limited substantive engagement has occurred behind the scenes. Importantly, it also means that Pacific-led ideas are not prioritised.

Pacific leaders or their nominated officials deserve to have a central role in the design, approval and delivery of Australian initiatives in the region. They deserve to know the purpose of initiatives before they are approved, how feedback can be provided and how this feedback will be considered by the Australian government.

It is in Australia's interests to be close to the Pacific. The region is crucial to Australia's security and economic prosperity. Maintaining relationships of trust – where Pacific governments are treated as equals in decisions that affect them – is one of the most important tools we have for ensuring a stable region.

THE PROPOSAL: Australia should place shared decision-making at the centre of its practice in the Pacific, by ensuring that its own pre-budget processes, where important decisions are made about policies and programs impacting Pacific lives, require the formal involvement of Pacific governments. Doing so will improve outcomes for Pacific governments, communities and people. It will also establish a more consistent and formal process of shared decision-making with Pacific governments.

Modernising Australia's budget and development program decision-making processes to ensure the stronger involvement of Pacific governments might seem difficult, but it is worth pursuing if we want our Pacific partners to be more involved in the policies and programs that affect their lives. In the 2025–26 budget, Australia allocated $2.157 billion in Official Development Assistance to the Pacific, representing a significant portion of its total foreign aid spending. Decisions made in Canberra about how this money is spent reverberate across the region.

Officials from the Department of Foreign Affairs and Trade do not need to look far to appreciate how this mode of engagement can work in Australia's favour. Shared decision-making is a cornerstone of Australia's approach to working with Aboriginal and Torres Strait Islander bodies on key policy areas under the National Agreement on Closing the Gap. Arrangements exist to enable Commonwealth government agencies to partner closely with representatives from the Coalition of Peaks – a representative group of more than eighty Aboriginal and Torres Strait Islander bodies – in developing new policy proposals.

For example, in March 2025, Australia's Department of Education signed a partnership agreement with SNAICC – National Voice for Our Children and the National Aboriginal and Torres Strait Islander Education Corporation (NATSIEC) to transform the way it works with those bodies to improve educational outcomes, from early childhood to higher education. The agreement commits the department to share decision-making with both SNAICC – National Voice for Our Children and NATSIEC on initiatives affecting Aboriginal and Torres Strait Islander children and their families. This is an example of Aboriginal and Torres Strait Islander leaders having a seat at the table in helping to inform the scope of new government programs before they move through formal budget approval processes.

Similar arrangements should be established with Pacific governments to deepen shared decision-making processes across key pillars of Australia's development program, in areas such as health, education, governance and policing. Adopting this way of working will ensure that Pacific leaders and officials have a formal means of regularly and directly engaging with senior Australian government officials – as equals – to make submissions to inform development funding decisions by the Australian government or to vet new funding ideas and opportunities identified by Australia before those proposals enter the budget cycle.

WHY IT WILL WORK: Adopting a more collaborative way of initiating, approving and implementing programs that affect Pacific people will improve Australia's engagement in the Pacific, add a respectful layer to Australia's regional relationships and strengthen our diplomatic ties. Initiating pre-budget engagement processes will make Australia the only country globally to have a shared decision-making model built into its foreign policy practices.

Domestically, the Australian government conducts pre-budget consultations with external partners. These consultations require good judgement, trust and, frequently, non-disclosure agreements. They are thus not without challenges, but the benefits of embracing these practices far outweigh the risks.

Pre-budget engagement naturally requires governments to relinquish a degree of control to come to decisions by consensus with external representatives. This is an uncomfortable space for officials and practitioners to operate in, but there is a strong realist argument for embracing this way of working. The Aboriginal and Torres Strait Islander education sector shows how this can be done.

In his 2018 "Reflections" on his 2001 book *After Victory,* John Ikenberry reminds readers of the legitimacy costs when leading powers resist opportunities to exercise self-restraint. Australia's strategy in the Pacific might have greater impact – and more regional support – if it accepts the utility of strategic restraint in this way. To forge a more durable model of cooperation in the Pacific, in which Australian and Pacific interests are mutually served, Australia should offer more opportunities for shared leadership across multiple initiatives with Pacific governments, including on policing.

The current gap between Australia's words and deeds on "Pacific-led" initiatives can be addressed. And we have examples at home showing how it can be done. ■

Reviews

The New India: The Unmaking of the World's Largest Democracy
Rahul Bhatia
Little, Brown

This ambitious, fluently written book sets out its aim on page five: "This book is … an attempt to see the roots of Hindutva, the unbending ideology of Hindu extremism … to find … where the poison is coming from."

The New India is a very personal exploration of why members of this talented journalist's family transformed their political beliefs, and of how the government of Narendra Modi and his Bharatiya Janata Party (BJP) won wide support and put India firmly on the road to becoming a Hindu-supremacist state.

Rahul Bhatia divides the book into five chapters, each dealing with a different facet of his attempt to answer the question, "Where is the poison coming from?" "Aftermath", the first and longest chapter, refers to the fallout from the riots and killing in Delhi that began in December 2019 and extended into the first months of 2020. The conflict resulted from the BJP government's legislating a *Citizenship (Amendment) Act* that gave Hindus, Sikhs, Parsees, Jains, Buddhists and Christians coming from Afghanistan, Bangladesh or Pakistan a pathway to Indian citizenship. Muslims, who account for 200 million of India's 1.4 billion people, were excluded, even though Ahmadiyyas, Sufis and political dissidents in the three neighbouring countries also face oppression.

The citizenship act is intended to contribute in future to a promised National Register of Citizens. To prove they are eligible to be registered, even people born in India may need documents. Muslim Indians saw the citizenship act and the proposed register as attempts to curtail their rights as citizens, including their right to vote.

In the resulting protests, especially at two universities in Delhi and in a suburb with a large Muslim population in the north-east of the city, vigilantes, unhindered by the police, attacked demonstrators. A local hospital was flooded with the wounded. Caught up in the mayhem, Bhatia encountered Nisar, a modestly prosperous Muslim businessman, who had most of his stock and equipment destroyed by vigilantes. Nisar was determined to press charges against the group that attacked him and his neighbours and doggedly attended court hearings as a witness. He and his wife, Asma, Bhatia writes, "are two of the bravest people I've known". Following Nisar to the courts, Bhatia met supporters and lawyers of the accused, usually members of groups affiliated with the BJP.

In the second chapter, "A New Country", Bhatia sets out to discover the historical foundations of the organised, propagated hatred of Muslims that he now sees around him. After the British subjugated most of India in the nineteenth century, European missionaries began to convert Indians to Christianity. Missionaries mocked Hindu beliefs, offered opportunities through English education and had – or so it appeared – a disciplined and united cadre of full-time workers in their priest and pastors.

By the beginning of World War I, Hindu organisations were attempting to adapt the missionaries' techniques to retain adherents and demonstrate a "modern" way of being Hindu. Later, the attractions of Italian fascism and Hitler's Nazis influenced the Hindu Mahasabha (founded in 1918) and the Rashtriya Swayamsevak Sangh (RSS, founded in 1925). Bhatia interviews scholars and writers who have researched or were members of organisations whose goal is the creation of a Hindu-ruled state that embodies their vision of what it means to be a Hindu.

The last landmark in Bhatia's quest for the foundations of today's beliefs and doctrines lies in the bloody transfer of populations during the partition of India and Pakistan in 1947. Ghastly memories have fuelled the zeal that keeps the RSS alive. The propagation and embellishment of such memories underpins the ideological foundation for Bhatia's answer to the question: "Where does the hate come from?"

The "family" in "Family Matters" (Chapter 3) can stand for the Sangh parivar, the RSS "family", an expression that includes groups aligned with the RSS. The "family" provides the flesh-and-blood memory, grievance and rebirth that drives the RSS and its movement. Bhatia does what he does so well: interviews, listens, takes notes and discovers the stories of true believers and an ex-believer.

"Technical Difficulties", the fourth chapter, emphasises the capacity of the digital world to subvert democracy and relentlessly purvey well-packaged messages of hate. Bhatia's focus is the Aadhaar, a digital identification number made possible through the rapid growth of smartphone availability. (*Aadhaar* means "foundation".)

The attraction of the Aadhaar ID is that it makes it easy for people to establish their identities and access government services. But the more information that is loaded onto the ID, the better the state can track the bearer. During riots, those who have access to the ID, legally or otherwise, have an effective tool to pinpoint people for the attention of vigilantes.

The successful advocate of the Aadhaar idea, which has been around since the early 2000s, was Nandan Nilekani, the billionaire co-founder of Infosys. He converted Narendra Modi to the idea after the BJP came to power in 2014. Despite court challenges, which Bhatia discusses at length, the scheme has grown rapidly. In March 2025, the Aadhaar dashboard showed 1.41 billion IDs, indicating that there are plenty of duplicates or "false positives". Though the ID is supposed to be voluntary, it is "mandatory voluntary" because many businesses demand it, even though they are not required to do so. Bhatia himself had to succumb and get an Aadhaar ID in order to maintain the bank account he'd been using for fourteen years.

For Bhatia, Nandan Nilekani has been a digital Mephistopheles, creating through Aadhaar the conditions in which the proposed National Register of Citizens and voting eligibility can be centralised in a single ID. The conditions are created in which an individual's rights of citizenship can be established, denied or removed with a few keystrokes.

In the final chapter, "An Education", Bhatia links up again with Nisar, the businessman, in the courtroom where Nisar is a key witness in the never-ending trial of the Hindu vigilantes accused of crimes in the riots of 2020. Bhatia has long interviews with the BJP lawyer defending the accused and discovers the deeply believed yet fanciful ideas that direct the man's life.

In the last vignette, Bhatia accompanies Nisar to his village in western Uttar Pradesh, 400 kilometres from Delhi. Nisar was lyrical about the purity of life in the village – the food, the air, the water, the people. As they were preparing to leave, a nephew he was fond of appeared and was ebullient at having helped a candidate win an election – but the candidate, to Nisar's surprise, was from the BJP. As they left the village, "there was a very particular look on [Nisar's] face", Bhatia writes. "It was a look that said: Perhaps it was not as I remembered." The village was now part of "the new India".

As Bhatia warns readers at the start, his book "is a reported elegy". It's an elegy for India's brave, flawed attempt in its first sixty-five years of independence to build a modern, democratic nation-state out of a vastly diverse population – out of many, one. It is a moving lament for an idea that will be hard to resurrect after more than ten years of "the new India".

Robin Jeffrey

Melanesia: Travels in Black Oceania
Hamish McDonald
Black Inc.

Hamish McDonald's *Melanesia: Travels in Black Oceania* is addressed to the "non-specialist" and intends to introduce them to the incredibly diverse cultures and societies that exist on the islands and atolls to the north-east of Australia. Towards the end of this journey, the author asks James Marape, Prime Minister of Papua New Guinea, what drives him. McDonald suggests that this "soft" line of questioning encourages his subject "to think beyond their current talking points". Marape responds on cue, with an account of his childhood in a village that has no electricity or sealed road yet is just thirty minutes away from one of this planet's most lucrative gold and copper mines.

Negotiating the tensions between traditional ways of life and a global modernity driven by capital is a theme to which we return over and over as we travel with McDonald from his home in Australia to Fiji, Vanuatu, New Caledonia, Solomon Islands and Bougainville, and then through Papua New Guinea and West Papua, back to the Torres Strait Islands and to Queensland, with its little-known history of Pacific slavery. McDonald imparts a wealth of detail around key events and individuals, taking his readers into a range of crucial histories and issues, from the arrival of Christianity to the coming of foreign mining companies.

However, most of the individuals, communities and nations whom we encounter are presented – as we are familiar with from Australian newspapers – as struggling and ultimately failing to prosper in a "modern" world of global connectivity and economic opportunity. Either that or they are actively exploiting their power and position at the expense of others. The rich connections that many of these individuals and communities have had with the land, sea, sky and culture of their ancestors are, it becomes clear as we turn the pages of *Melanesia*, tragically being lost.

I was recently introduced to the diaries and letters of the early-twentieth-century Swiss ethnologist Felix Speiser, who travelled to the northern Solomon Islands to document and collect what he believed were the last remnants of a culture and people on the brink of extinction. A lot of his language, inspired by evolutionary ideas of the time, is, to our contemporary ears, blatantly racist and deeply disturbing. In his preface McDonald responds critically to the racism inherent in such presentations and calls out the amassing – at times blatant theft – by national heroes such as photographer Frank Hurley of vast numbers of significant cultural material that would ultimately fill the storage facilities of Australian museums.

I mention these colonial agents and the impact of their published views, as we can no longer pretend to be untouched by colonialist assumptions and need to be mindful of the lens through which we (as foreign commenters) look at our island neighbours. How do we (I include myself) move beyond our own Pacific talking points and colonially learned perspectives as we try to approach the histories, culture and contemporary realities of our nearest island neighbours?

This is much harder than it sounds. I have just discarded a few hundred words that I had written for an earlier draft of this text. The draft was filled with observations about an artist with whom I have worked for many years creating new work – an example of how traditions continue to flourish in contemporary ways. I felt that the text sounded righteous and, in speaking about instead of with, had become an example of the pot calling the kettle black.

That is not where I want to go. But I do want to address the ways in which McDonald, and I, frame our own writing. As much as either of us might wish to foster greater understanding and appreciation of the rich contemporary cultures and issues facing our nearest neighbours, we continue to do this using language, dialectics and ideas that are not from those locales.

For example, I find McDonald's title, *Melanesia* – a colonially imposed word deriving from the ancient Greek terms for "dark" and "islands" – and his subtitle, with its focus on "Black" Oceania, quite provocative, as some are less than comfortable using the term "Black" to describe the region. Is McDonald being transparent, telling us from the get-go that his view of this region of diverse cultures is framed by a colonial perspective, an outsider's view? Or is it something less thought through?

While I appreciate the honesty and sense of justice that McDonald brings to his discussions of the destruction caused by colonialism and missionisation to societies and cultures across the region, I yearn for more about what continues to thrive from before and beyond this destruction. I think of the words of ni-Vanuatu writer and musician Marcel Melthérorong, imparting a creation story of the region that he gathered: "Stories of kings and queens departing from the Isa Tabu group of island by canoes led the caravan through Vanua Levu which will become the gate before the procession settle their kingdoms along the South

Pacific. Strangely, the northern side of the border from Isa Tabu is shared with the Taiwanese kingdom. So the guardians of the kings and queens will be strong and powerful to keep the border safe."

The poetry, literature and oral histories of the islands and atolls from Fiji to the Torres Strait abound with such insights and histories. No matter how self-reflexive we are, creating histories – which ultimately is what *Melanesia: Travels in Black Oceania* will become – that frame the region via colonial perspectives and encounters only perpetuates the authority of those perspectives. This needs to change.

The tension between traditional ways – or *kastom*, as McDonald calls it, although this Bislama term is not used indiscriminately across the region – and modernity is somehow at the crux of this. McDonald's text uses this tension to take the reader into the ways in which his subjects continue to negotiate the huge challenges that have resulted from the colonisation and missionisation of their homelands. He wants us to understand the impact of the imposition of our cultures. In doing this, he fails, in my opinion, to adequately demonstrate that *kastom* has always been alive and responsive to change, or the ways in which modern individuals continue to demonstrate a strong adherence to cultural values and worldviews. Kastom is not killed by change; it grows with it, in positive and sometimes not-so-positive ways. It always has.

I find myself returning to a review by the Sepik anthropologist Dr Andrew Moutu of Bernard Narokobi's *The Melanesian Way*. Moutu notes a dilemma that results from "the curious tension between 'tradition' and 'modernity'" that "newly independent nations often encounter" (and that is common, I would add, to commentators on them). Moutu outlines the ways in which Narokobi, a modern intellectual who helped pen the creation of an independent Papua New Guinea, refused to resort to either the cultural essentialism or epochalism (the viewing of culture as comprised of distinct epochs, one replacing the other) that we witness in so much literature about this region. In Moutu's words, Narokobi "didn't just defend traditional Melanesian values but actually claimed modernity not as a cultural predicament but as a Melanesian project".

Working with artists and communities from these islands over the past two decades, I have met many more individuals, community leaders, and grassroots and civil society organisations who adhere to the traditional Melanesian values of reciprocity and connection to their environment than otherwise. I have also seen more evidence of the vibrancy of contemporary culture than I see in any suburb in Australia. The project and process of realising a "Melanesian" modernity might not always look like one we understand or recognise, but it was never meant to. That is what I love about this region. I believe McDonald does too.

Ruth McDougall

Correspondence

"Continental gift: Trump and Australia's place in the world" by James Curran

Kathryn Paik

In "Continental Gift" (Australian Foreign Affairs 23), James Curran presents us with a choice: either Australia continues in its subservient relationship with the United States, whereby it offers its "gift of geography" to America's pursuit of confrontation with China, or Australia sheds its obsession with American ties, accepts the inevitable rise of China and works to craft its own place in that new architecture.

Both choices are misrepresentations of reality. They ignore Australia's agency as a nation, and the real and direct impact that Chinese ambitions have on Australian national security – even outside of a relationship with America. The drastic shift in Australia's policy towards China over the last decade has not simply been a decision to fall in line with its larger ally. It is informed in large part by China's actions in the region and within Australia. As argued in Australia's 2023 Defence Strategic Review, Chinese actions in Australia's near region directly threaten Australian security, requiring a shift from a "defence of Australia" doctrine to an approach that recognises Australia's critical role in the collective effort to safeguard international rules and norms.

Curran complains that there has not been any serious debate on whether Australia should align so fulsomely with the United States and provide it with offensive capabilities. This may be true, but if anything this debate must be taken several steps further. We must ask: what are Australia's national interests? How are they threatened? And how far is Australia willing to go to protect them?

For most Australian policymakers, the question about the threat has been answered – but perhaps this message has not been conveyed clearly enough to the public. Curran seems to recommend a more passive stance vis-à-vis China when he posits that the belief that China is hegemonic in nature is founded out of fear, rather than pointing to the numerous examples China has given us over the years of its ambition, desire and capacity to drastically alter global norms to fit its worldview (in other words, hegemony). Then, curiously, he asserts that China "will likely exercise that kind of hegemony over Australia anyway" – which seems to both acknowledge China's hegemonic ambitions and state that Australia should pre-emptively throw its hands in the air and give itself over to this new authoritarian hegemon. Or perhaps Curran simply believes that this China-led future will not be so bad? (Let's just ignore Hong Kong and Xinjiang, I suppose.)

Curran casts Australia as only a passive observer of great-power competition, rather than recognising that Australian interests are also being directly threatened by China. He states that "Australia is now involved in contingency planning for a war of undefined provocation or cause". Actually, Australia is preparing, in partnership with others, to deter conflict with (and, if needed, to mount defence against) a revisionist power that seeks to define rules and norms in ways that run counter to Australian interests.

Perhaps nothing today symbolises the US–Australian alliance like AUKUS, which might explain Curran's disdain for it. He clearly believes that AUKUS is a folly: he asserts that policymakers "must surely know, in their heart of hearts, that AUKUS will be a Potemkin" and that it was pursued primarily to forge deeper strategic alignment with America. And yet many might argue that AUKUS is the *result* of significant strategic alignment, and that the arrangement will bring unprecedented deterrence capability to Australia's shores – and directly into Australia's hands.

I agree with Curran that Trump's drastic about-face in foreign policy should give Australia pause. Australia's moves in recent years to strengthen its partnerships with likeminded nations in Asia such as the Philippines and Japan are logical and should continue. Curran refers to this in his note on how the "scatter and survive" policy complements the latticework of partnerships for which the United States has advocated in recent years. These policies create resilience, which in turn bolsters deterrence. Yet the United States' current warming to Russia and its unclear stance on China may prompt other nations to more fulsomely advocate for their own interests. Indeed, Australia has already shown a willingness to do so in the Pacific by crafting several bespoke bilateral agreements – in Nauru on banking, in Papua New Guinea on rugby league and in Tuvalu on immigration – that all included a security provision preventing Chinese inroads.

The author's assertion that Australia is "well placed" for Trump's second term, however, is overconfident. While Australia has much to point to when it comes to proving its worth to America – a solid history of partnership, a favourable trade balance (a rarity among allies) and defence spending just squeaking over 2 per cent of GDP – these facts, in the end, may not be enough to keep it out of the crosshairs of the transactionally minded Trump; indeed, it was not sufficient to avoid the base tariff rate of 10 per cent. Loyalty and history are no guarantee against pursuit of a better deal.

Should Australian leaders continually evaluate the alliance? Absolutely – perhaps even more so now. However, it is a mischaracterisation to say that prioritising the alliance ties Australia to US interests that are discordant with Australia's own security needs. Saying as much places Australia in the passive role of a smaller country at the whims of larger powers. It ignores the evolution of Australia's active role in the region, America's regard for that role and the very real danger posed by an expansionist Chinese state.

Kathryn Paik is a senior fellow and deputy director with the Australia Chair at the Center for Strategic and International Studies.

Courtney Stewart

In "Continental Gift", James Curran paints a picture of an Australia drifting dangerously close to becoming an uninformed launchpad of American war planning, driven by fears of alliance abandonment and risks of entanglement in a US strategy of Chinese containment. At the heart of his argument is a concern that Canberra is surrendering too much, too quietly and without the consent of the Australia people. While Curran raises important questions about public debate and democratic oversight, his conclusions risk reinforcing an outdated view of Australia's role in the region as passive. It's a view that misreads the purpose of force posture initiatives and underestimates the strategic logic behind our national security decisions.

Curran presents three tensions: first, that Australia lacks a meaningful national conversation about the benefits and risks of deepening US military cooperation; second, that this cooperation amounts to ceding territory for American warfighting, benefiting the United States at the expense of our own strategic freedom; and third, that such arrangements make us a target, potentially implicating Australia in conflicts we don't support. These are fair anxieties. But they are built on a narrow and at times cynical interpretation of Australia's agency, and they fail to account for the regional context, the logic of deterrence and the evolution of the US–Australian alliance into something more collective for the region.

Let's be clear: the United States was not imposed on Australia. The decision to deepen US access to Australian territory was not an act of desperation or dependence, but a conscious choice made across successive governments with bipartisan support. It reflects a shared understanding that Australia benefits when the United States remains present, engaged and relevant in the

Indo-Pacific. That presence isn't driven by US war planning – it supports deterrence, regional stability and the norms and conditions necessary for Australia's continued prosperity.

The argument that such cooperation makes Australia a target ignores the fact that we are already exposed by our geography, values and interests. The question is whether we face that exposure alone or as part of a credible, collective effort to deter coercion and manage regional competition (not only between great powers). The point of deterrence is not to be escalatory but to be continually calibrated to the threat in a way that persuades the other actor not to take an action you seek to prevent. Deterrence is stabilising and seeks to maintain the status quo. It reduces the risk of miscalculation by showing potential adversaries that the costs will be too high and that regional nations are neither isolated nor easily coerced. While deterrence is not a panacea, and is not guaranteed by capability alone, we will fail to deter credibly without a clear commitment to stand together, trust each other and demonstrate our collective strength.

Access isn't just about infrastructure, logistics and maintenance across ports, airfields and depots; it's also about training, exercising and building real operational coordination. Strengthening cooperation and interoperability directly supports collective deterrence. Curran fails to observe that Australian force posture is becoming increasingly multinational. Japan will soon begin rotating an Amphibious Rapid Deployment Brigade to northern Australia to cooperate with the Australian Defence Force and the US Marines. I expect Japanese F-35 fighter jet deployments will follow. Australia is building a coalition-based ecosystem. This is not simply about the United States defending Australia, it's about Australia shaping an alliance and partnership network and a regional order to reflect our interests. And in that order, access and cooperation are currencies of influence.

If we want the great power to consider our interests when the pressure is on, we need to be in the room, bringing capability, geography and commitment to the table. Those are the trade-offs middle powers make to be strategic actors, not spectators or targets. Yes, Australia should and does have a say in allied planning for combined operations. If a unilateral US decision were made to respond to a crisis using Australian territory, such action should require Australian consent, through full knowledge and concurrence.

Overall, Curran's concern about the absence of public debate is valid. We suffer from a persistent failure to articulate a coherent strategic narrative that links the security threats we face to Australia's national interests to defence policy, posture and capability requirements. Without it, the public is left wondering why we're making long-term military investments, what risks we're really managing and what trade-offs may be necessary. That failure of communication doesn't invalidate the logic of the decisions themselves but it certainly makes them harder to sustain politically.

Australia is not a gift. We are a capable, sovereign actor choosing to contribute to regional stability in a time of uncertainty. And that contribution must be understood not as deference but as a choice, both now under Trump 2.0 and into the future.

Courtney Stewart is a resident senior fellow at the Australian Strategic Policy Institute and a former US Department of Defense (DoD) policy exchange officer to the Australian DoD.

Charles Miller

They may not have said so publicly, but the leaders of America's allies, from Ottawa, Kyiv and London to Seoul, Paris and Tokyo, were quietly praying that tens of thousands of swing-state residents would cast their votes for Kamala Harris last November. On reflection, this is a strange and frankly demeaning way to run one's national security policy – hoping that a small number of voters in a foreign country will opt for one candidate rather than another in an election that will be decided on issues that have nothing to do with you.

The official line coming out of America's allies, including Australia, is that it does not matter who is in the White House – our relations with America will remain "unbreakable", as James Curran puts it. But the initial months of the Trump presidency gave the lie to this diplomatic fiction. Kamala Harris would not have started a worldwide trade war or discussed annexing Canada and Greenland, nor would she have suspended military aid to Ukraine while teaming up with her vice president to berate Volodymyr Zelenskyy for an alleged lack of gratitude and talking up the "amazing opportunities" of a new business relationship with Russia. Bluntly, in this historical era, America's allies can rely on America if and only if a Democrat is in the White House. Since a Democrat is not in the White House now, and we cannot rely on one being there in future, this means that we cannot rely on America full stop.

So what are we Australians to do?

On the surface, there seem to be good reasons for Australia not to panic about the Trump administration. While many erstwhile US allies have come under fire, multiple senior administration figures have underlined America's commitment to Australian security and the AUKUS pact, from Vice President

J.D. Vance to Secretary of Defense Pete Hegseth. Australia offers the United States a number of valuable assets, from Pine Gap to forward bases much closer to potential conflict zones in the Asia-Pacific. AUKUS is a deal almost perfectly crafted to appeal to Donald Trump's sensibilities: Australia pays the United States large sums of money to help it recapitalise its industrial base, in return for which the United States might, at some future date, give us some submarines.

These factors are bolstered by one theory of the Trump administration's grand strategy. Perhaps Trump is moving closer to Russia in order to pull it away from an alignment with China. Besides undermining Chinese power, such a gambit would allow the United States to divert its forces and attention away from Europe and towards the main theatre of competition in the Asia-Pacific. A more moderate version of this idea is not that the United States would align with Russia but rather deprioritise it – if Europe consequently rearms, US forces will no longer be required to deter Russia and can be shifted to the Asia-Pacific. The latter option was outlined in detail by Trump's under secretary of defense for policy, Elbridge Colby, in his 2021 book *The Strategy of Denial*. If this is indeed Trump's intent, Australia can live with it or even benefit from it, though it does not suit the Europeans and would be disastrous for Ukraine.

But there is a darker interpretation of Trump's moves. This is the idea that he wishes to divide the world into discrete spheres of influence between the great powers – whom he envisages as Russia, China and the United States. This idea was dubbed the "Metternich-Lindbergh Theory" by American economist Noah Smith. In this scenario, the United States might simply wash its hands of Australia and hand it over to the Chinese sphere of influence.

The broader point, however, is that it doesn't matter all that much. Even if we assume that the Trump administration sincerely intends to balance Chinese power in the Asia-Pacific, its policies are undermining this goal. The combination of perceived flakiness on defence with extractive trade wars and protectionism will push many Asia-Pacific states into the Chinese column. Moreover, as Smith, former deputy secretary of state Kurt Campbell and political scientist Rush Doshi all point out, matching Chinese industrial power over the long run would require integrating all of America's Asia-Pacific allies into one large, seamless single market to benefit from the economies of scale that China enjoys by itself. Trump's protectionism is ruling this out.

Zooming out, I am not confident that the fundamental weaknesses that Trump has exposed in the US political system will be patched up anytime soon. As Curran writes, some in Canberra "will simply close their eyes to Trump, hoping to find something more familiar when they awaken four years later". This would be a mistake, just as it was in 2020. The problem is that the guardrails that once prevented unsuitable or downright dangerous presidential candidates – from Pat Buchanan to Herman Cain – from gaining office have gone. In the past, party elites ensured that such figures were denied their party's nomination. Even if some wayward demagogue slipped through, American voters of old rejected them – as they did Barry Goldwater in 1964. Now, however, the American public is so polarised that the majority will vote for their party's candidate no matter what, and elections are swung by a handful of voters driven by macroeconomic indicators that are a deceptive measure of an incumbent administration's actual quality. As long as this is the case, America's allies simply cannot rely on the United States not to elect a president at least as damaging as Donald Trump.

Charles Miller is a senior lecturer in politics and international relations at the Australian National University.

James Curran responds

At the invitation of the editor of Australian Foreign Affairs, I have put together a brief commentary on the three responses to my essay "Continental Gift". The first point to make is that two of the responses, by Kathryn Paik and Courtney Stewart, do not address the question of how Trump's return to the White House in 2025 fits into broader historical debates over Australia's place in the world. This failure to understand my approach renders nugatory any attempt to produce a meaningful conversation. It would also be worth knowing if the two authors would reconsider their response in light of the developments in Washington since Trump's inauguration, as their critiques appear mostly oblivious to the wrecking ball the American president has swung through cherished assumptions about US global leadership and, in particular, the US alliance system. Paik concedes, almost as an afterthought, that "[l]oyalty and history are no guarantee against pursuit of a better deal" with a transactional Trump, but her response, along with Stewart's, could have been written some years ago. In their own way, both responses reassert the orthodox interpretation of recent Australian foreign and defence policy: that China poses an existential threat to Australian security, and that as a result there should be no limits to Canberra's support for the US alliance.

The response from Charles Miller, however, recognises the serious questions arising from Trump's first months in office, particularly for the subject of American reliability. Miller's thoughtful and measured analysis, written before Trump's decision on tariffs, makes the point that Washington's "perceived flakiness on defence [and] extractive trade wars and protectionism will push many Asia-Pacific states into the Chinese column". Trump, he argues, may well be thinking about dividing the world into discrete spheres of influence between the United States, Russia and China, in which the US might "wash its hands of Australia", leaving it to find its way in Beijing's world. Miller has articulated the strategic nightmare of the current generation of Australian policymakers. Unlike the other respondents, he confronts squarely the impacts of a changed America.

My essay raised questions about the extent and reach of US–Australian military integration over the last twenty-five years. It also argued that the long-term dynamic at the heart of Australian foreign policy since the 19th century – the tension between its cultural loyalty to a great-power protector and its distinctive national interests arising from its position on the edge of Asia – may have reached a denouement. Prior to 1996, this clash between culture and interests produced many instances of creative middle-power diplomacy. Now, however, the reappearance of an Asian great power has revived the need for intense reliance on the United States and, since the Howard era, all Australian governments have lined up to give America a greater military presence in the country. They have done so out of a longstanding and chronic anxiety that the ANZUS guarantee may well not hold. And so deep now is the integration between US and Australian military forces, so rusted on is Canberra to "alliance maintenance", that the relationship could only be unstitched with some difficulty, and with substantial consequences for Australia's society and its relaxed form of government.

Both Paik and Stewart, who fail to acknowledge the cultural dimension of foreign relations, reduce my argument to one about Australian "passivity". They claim the emphasis I placed on the consequences of an increased US presence for Australian sovereign decision-making is tantamount to a betrayal of Australian "agency". But their evidence for this "agency" is the well-worn example of hedging and diversification, most often manifest in the view that Canberra's membership of the Quad and its pursuit of closer military relations with Japan, the Philippines and other regional partners constitute a distinctively Australian response to the prospect of a region absent America. The point, though, as I have often made in my columns for the *Australian Financial Review*, is that the current government speaks with a forked tongue. It talks of a region "where no one country dominates", to quote Foreign Minister Penny Wong, but both its search for "strategic equilibrium" in the region and its calls for respect of "ASEAN centrality" are built upon the premise that US primacy should be maintained.

Paik presents the most egregiously reductionist interpretation of my argument, echoing a line that has been used and abused by China hawks for almost a decade – namely, that to question the alliance in any way is tantamount to endorsing Xi Jinping's sabre-rattling in the South China Sea and elsewhere. Paik alleges, without foundation, that my argument amounts to a choice between further US and Australian military integration and a blithe acceptance of Chinese hegemony. My article made no such claim and offered no such "choice". Paik fails to acknowledge that, for all Australia's loud claims to the contrary, the reality is that great powers – first Britain, then America – have often played fast and loose with Australian interests. How else to interpret deputy secretary of state Kurt Campbell's quip that Australia's AUKUS submarines, if ever delivered, "won't be lost" to America? Or national security advisor Jake Sullivan's assumption that the same agreement amounts to a "fifty-year marriage" between the two countries? For much of the alliance's history, Washington has treated Canberra as if it can be either dominated or ignored.

There do, however, appear to be some points of convergence. All three responses support my contention concerning the lack of genuine public debate about the strategic choices Australia has taken in relation to the alliance over the last fifteen years. This is as true of the decision by the Gillard government to accept the presence of US marines in Darwin in 2011 as it is of Scott Morrison's 2021 announcement on AUKUS. To these decisions Anthony Albanese and his national security colleagues in cabinet have only added a deafening silence. The absence of Australian political leadership on this question only intensifies the broader doubts circulating about the nation's strategic direction, especially given the cast of crusaders and cranks now holding power in Washington.

James Curran is Professor of Modern History at the University of Sydney and a foreign affairs columnist for the Australian Financial Review.

The Back Page

FOREIGN POLICY CONCEPTS AND JARGON, EXPLAINED

GLOBAL SWING STATES

What is it: A term that refers to countries that are influential but have not taken sides in the United States–China rivalry. Jared Cohen (fellow, Council on Foreign Relations) says global swing states are "critical to the world economy and balance of power, but they don't have the capacity by themselves to drive the global agenda, at least for now".

Who coined it: Ashley J. Tellis (senior associate, Carnegie Endowment for International Peace) described India in 2005 as the world's most important "swing state", adapting the label used for American states whose political allegiances can shift at presidential elections. In 2012, Daniel M. Kliman (fellow, German Marshall Fund) and Richard Fontaine (president, Center for a New American Security) expanded the term, urging the US to partner with four "global swing states": Brazil, India, Indonesia and Turkey.

Who's in: Saudi Arabia, South Africa, Mexico, Nigeria, Vietnam and Argentina have been labelled swing states. Australia, which is US-aligned and geographically remote, has not.

Who likes it: Advocates say the US and Europe must focus on engaging with swing states as China and Russia become more assertive. Cliff Kupchan (chair, Eurasia Group) says swing states are "regional leaders, and they become more important as power devolves to their regions".

Who doesn't: Critics say so-called swing states may not actually be willing to swing. Zeno Leoni and Sarah Tzinieris (academics, King's College London) have argued that Washington, Beijing and Moscow lack the diplomatic prowess to forge alliances with swing states, noting that "smaller powers may be hard to influence geopolitically owing to local security and political priorities".